AF215300

PERFECT PARENTING

Sushant Kalra, a father of two, is the founder of the Parwarish Institute of Parenting. His professional experience of over 28 years spans across the Manufacturing, Venture Capital Financing, Banking, Insurance and Education & Training industries. He has trained over 8000 employees in various Change Management, Process Optimization and new Process projects. Parwarish has trained over 18000 parents and more than 25000 teachers across the world. Parwarish has won several awards for its work, including the Best Teacher and Parent Coach Award from the Federation of Public Schools of Delhi, the Education INNOVATOR Award at the 5th Ed Leadership International Conference, from The Center For Innovation in Education, USA and the Courageous Class award conferred by the Kenneth Cole Foundation USA.

PERFECT PARENTING

How To Raise Happy
And Successful Children

SUSHANT KALRA

RUPA

Published by
Rupa Publications India Pvt. Ltd 2021
161-B/4, Gulmohar House,
Yusuf Sarai Community Centre,
New Delhi 110049

Sales centres:
Bengaluru Chennai
Hyderabad Kolkata Mumbai

P-ISBN: 978-93-89967-67-8
E-ISBN: 978-93-89967-68-5

Fourteenth impression 2025

20 19 18 17 16 15 14

The moral right of the author has been asserted.

Printed in India

CONTENTS

FOREWORD

Such a book was long overdue. It is a well-known fact that a child's future personality gets influenced enormously by what she sees at home. Hence, there is a need to make a conscious effort to present to the child an environment that allows and enables her to evolve as an individual who looks at the world positively.

Sushant doesn't forcibly impose his ideas, which are so logically outlined in the book. He first looks at the rationale for appropriate parenting. He believes that parenting is critical and presents a very compelling case. He induces the reader to think, to ponder and to introspect about their own parenting style. There is an attempt to understand what parents really want for their children. This constitutes the analytical part of the book. The major portion of the book is dedicated to exploring how one can evolve as a mature parent who can influence the lives of their children in a positive and nurturing manner. In doing so, Sushant goes on to burst various myths which we have believed in for a long time, such as the generation gap, being unable to see who a child really is, inability to understand the world of children and teens etc.

Sushant's objective is clear—the welfare of the child. But the focus is on the parents. They have to set an example and not merely preach. A child is extremely perceptive. She may not appear so, but she sees through all that is 'dished' out. Hence, the conduct of the parents assumes prime importance.

There are also concrete suggestions on offer regarding what the author calls 'screen detox'. Eating healthy food is a habit that can and should be inculcated by the parents, and this book details how you can do so for your child. And, finally, Sushant talks about 'finding balance' while you unveil the real definition of parenting.

This is a practical guide that covers children of all age groups, from toddlers to young adults. The case studies of families give an insight into how these tools have been implemented by families over these years

A book worth reading, worth keeping, and the ideas, worth imbibing.

Anil Swarup

Anil Swarup, IAS 1981 batch;
Served as:
Education Secretary of India,
Coal Secretary of India,
Additional Secretary in the Cabinet Secretariat of India,
Additional Secretary of Labour & Empowerment,
Export Commissioner in the Ministry of Commerce & Industry of India;
Author, 'not just a Civil Servant'

PROLOGUE

You may have picked up this book to find a solution to a problem you are facing with your child, or for some parenting tips. You may be an expectant parent, or your child may already be a young adult. Wherever you are in your parenting journey, this book will help you expand your knowledge of parenting and your self-awareness as a parent.

In the words of Elizabeth Stone: 'Making the decision to have a child—it is momentous. It is to decide forever to have your heart go walking around outside your body.' And this certainly can not be easy. Leave alone the health and future of our children—even the slightest of bruises can cause a lot of anxiety for us. As parents, we perhaps feel the pain of our children's hurts more than them. We won't sleep a wink when our little prince or princess is unwell.

Have they eaten well? Have they eaten healthy? Have they had enough sleep? These and many more such questions plague the minds of parents day and night. Our paediatrician had rightly informed us when our son Aman was three months old that our worrying for him would never cease—not even five decades later! Worrying about a child is a lifelong phenomenon for any parent; the only thing that changes is what we worry about and how we project it outwardly.

So much for being a parent! What about parenting? We have often heard that there is no manual for it. That every parent has to figure out things on their own as they go along. That it's a trial and error process, and that it varies for each person. That in the end, everything will turn out just fine. But does it really work that way? If we introspect closely, don't we find ourselves still carrying the baggage of our childhood—the self-doubts and the 'what ifs'? What if Dad had done this or not done that? What if Mom had handled that situation differently for me? What if... We never really get past those 'what ifs', and perhaps even try to make up for them when it comes to parenting our own children.

While we do have our own experiences as children to fall back on, we cannot ignore the fact that each individual is different—not just in terms of thoughts, feelings and emotions, but also in how they react to any given situation or experience. So our parenting techniques, which are often culminations of our learning from our own parents' approaches in terms of dealing—or not dealing—with situations their way, may or may not work with our children. Have you noticed how your parents' approach impacted you and your siblings differently? Clearly, no single approach to parenting can be adopted by even a single set of parents for all their children, let alone by different sets of parents for different sets of children in different generations.

So, maybe we *do* need a parenting manual. Look no further, for this is *that* parenting manual for you. It can help you on your parenting journey. All you need to do is experience it—don't just read this book, but adopt its recommendations in your life as a parent. Adopt, practise, implement, execute—those are key to making the best use of this parenting manual.

You may read this book cover to cover at first, and later come back to the relevant portions when facing a dilemma. And if at any point you have larger questions that you need help with beyond this book, Parwarish is just a call away.

WHY LEARN PARENTING[*]

You may be thinking: 'I know my child and our situation the best. How can someone else, who has not experienced what we are going through, tell me what to do?'

Let's look at this question more closely and from different perspectives:

- We need to learn almost every skill that we acquire—from languages and different subjects at school, to cooking, driving and sports. But when it comes to parenting, we think it will come naturally. Why is that so?
- If we know everything about parenting, why do our children still face issues?
- When we say we know all about parenting, are we discarding the possibility of a better approach to it?

When we talk of this book being a parenting manual, we do not mean that it will provide absolute, readymade solutions to your problems. It will instead give you tools to aid you. Focus on and be in the process and you will be creating your own solutions, which will help you and your child move ahead whenever you find yourselves at crossroads.

---

[*] https://www.youtube.com/watch?v=rex8RLdGaxo

The manual will teach you the alphabets of parenting; it will teach you the grammar—how to build words and sentences. From there, it is up to you how you want to use the language of parenting in your life.

Now that we know the importance of being open to learning parenting, the question that's most likely to come up is—at what age do we learn parenting? Some of you may say that parenting is to be learnt when you are about to become parents. Some may see it as an ongoing process which continues even when your child is a young adult, and perhaps even beyond that. A few of you may even say that the learning process begins when you are a child yourself—and that is true. We start picking up lessons on parenting quite young—from as early as when we are five or six years old. There were things our parents did that we liked, and then there were some actions or communications from them that hurt us. Over the years, we started formulating our parenting style. For example, if my father was a strict disciplinarian and his style of being a stickler for discipline didn't work for me, I would rebel, and it would impact my relationship with him. It could create a couple of persistent thoughts in my brain. One, too much discipline doesn't work and can push a child to rebel and two, a longing for a good, intimate relationship with the father.

Over our growing-up years, we collect a lot of similar experiences and make inferences, formulating parenting styles of our own even before we become parents ourselves. We consider these parenting styles to be reliable, for who can refute something steeped in experience? But we forget one critical thing: our parenting styles are based on *our* experience, and our children are not us. Our children are different individuals with their own separate ways of thinking and feeling, their own sets of emotions and reactions. Moreover, we and our children were born in different eras, and what worked more than two decades ago may not work in the current environmental and societal conditions.

If we look around us closely, we will find that the following problems are rampant in our country and also in the world at large:

- Alcoholism among children is increasing every year.
- Substance abuse is rampant in schools.
- The average age at which children become sexually active is decreasing with each passing year. According to a 2016 *Times of India* report, the average age was 14 years then.
- Divorce rates are increasing every year.
- Psychosomatic diseases like headaches, stomach aches and depression are surfacing more often and at an earlier age.

If parenting was a natural process and did not need to be learnt—if we were indeed better than our parents—then the overall situation in society would be improving and the world at large would have been a better place to live in. Since it isn't so, there is definitely a piece that is missing from the parenting jigsaw puzzle: what we need is not a parenting style based on our personal experiences, but one that is child-centric. Such a style can help realize the unlimited potential of our children, which otherwise remains untapped—or trapped—under the impact of the environment in which they grow up.

This book is a step towards adopting that child-centric approach to parenting. I would like to thank you for picking up this book and congratulate you for taking the first step towards a much-needed shift in your understanding of parenting. The actions that follow are going to make a real difference to your children's lives.

Happy reading—and implementing—this new approach to parenting in your lives!

2

THE COMMON ISSUES

Over the last 10 years, Parwarish has been partnering with and empowering parents of children of all age groups. Parents—whether they are parents of a two-year-old or a 25-year-old—have been coming to us with the objective of learning to resolve the issues between their children and them, and taking that relationship to the next level.

The most common issues faced by parents can be found in the list below:

- Eating habits
  - It's so difficult to feed him.
  - We have to put on the TV or the iPad to feed her.
  - She doesn't eat any vegetables.
  - He never finishes his food.
  - He only eats when I feed him with my own hands.
  - I have to chase him around the house to feed him.
  - She gets lost in her thoughts and mealtimes last for an entire hour.
- Screen addiction
  - They are always glued to the screen.
  - They are getting aggressive. The games they play depict violence and use inappropriate language.
  - One day I got up and saw him on the phone. It was

2 a.m. and he had school that day.

- He is always on social media. It takes up so much of his time. He has even stopped going to his friend's place.
- Getting them to go for their hobby classes/sports is an effort.

- Studies
  - Getting her to do her homework is a task. Even at 9.30 p.m. she says she will do it. Sometimes I have to literally drag her out at bedtime.
  - He hid his class test marks from me. He kept saying that the teacher hadn't yet returned the test papers. It was only when I bumped into his classmate's mother that I came to know about it.
  - His scores are falling. He is good, but he just does not put in effort. His teacher also says that he has huge potential, but he is not putting in enough effort.
  - She does not sit still at her desk in her class. She roams around the class when the teacher is teaching. The school wants us to take her to a counsellor and get her assessed for attention deficit.
  - He does so well when I am teaching him at home, but he answers incorrectly in his exams.
  - Tuitions have stopped impacting him. He avoids going for them.
  - We are receiving a lot of complaints from his school regarding his behaviour.
  - The school counsellor is asking us to get him assessed for learning disability.

- Communication
  - They do not communicate; they don't share their world with us.
  - She wants to spend all her time alone in her room.
  - I have no idea what is going on in his head.
  - They appear to be very moody and upset.
  - Is he in the right company?
- Sibling rivalry
  - We cannot leave them together without supervision for even five minutes.
  - They both want the same thing at the same time. Neither of them is willing to understand and relent.
  - I have to assume the role of an adjudicator all the time.
  - He accuses me of loving his brother more than him.
- Sexuality
  - They are exposed to porn so early.
  - Reading about incidents of child sexual abuse in the newspapers makes me paranoid about her safety.
  - I just cannot bear to let them out of my sight. It is so unsafe out there. I cannot even send them alone to tuitions.
  - Children are experimenting with sex at an early age. This worries me about their physical and emotional safety.
  - Sex has become a very casual topic even for preteens; one they may find normal to indulge in.
- Substance abuse
  - The availability of these materials makes me feel worried.

- o Smoking, drinking and weed have become style statements. Children are experimenting.
- Peer pressure
  - o She wants an iPhone at this young an age.
  - o I cannot go and pick him up in a smaller car.
  - o The birthday party location has to be decided by him.
  - o Even though he is just four years old, he wants to buy branded clothes.
- Behavioural issues
  - o She doesn't talk to elders with respect.
  - o He does exactly the opposite of what we ask him to do.
  - o She always talks back. She has an opinion about everything and doesn't want to listen to or understand our point of view. It feels very disrespectful.
  - o She doesn't care about how others feel; she should learn to get along with everyone.
  - o Of late he's become very insensitive.
  - o There is too much aggression in him. Talking in a loud and aggressive tone has become a norm.
- Dressing and self-image
  - o She has a very different dressing sense; her clothes seem to be very inappropriate on occasions.
  - o He is too much of a show-off.
  - o The pursuit of fashion and looking good is impacting her health.
  - o He takes too long to get ready.
- Not taking responsibility of their belongings
  - o His school bag, shoes, uniform are thrown all over the place; I need to run around and clean up after him.

○ She never puts her stuff back in its place.
○ The washroom is in a mess after he's used it. He doesn't care how it's left after his usage.

You may find a few of these resonating with you. Or maybe your concerns are very different from the ones on this list. The list is not exhaustive. Don't worry if your specific concern does not appear in it; the processes laid down in this book will help you resolve even those concerns that aren't listed here.

When we talk to parents around us and find that most of us are dealing with these issues, we start taking the issues for granted—we start accepting them as normal, as things that are bound to happen, as the ways of the world. We resign ourselves to them. But there are solutions. So, don't be disheartened. Read on…

3

KNOW YOUR PARENTING STYLE

The first step, as we embark on this journey to reassess our approach to parenting, is to identify our existing parenting style. Each one of us has their own style of parenting and a lot of research has been done on the various styles. While the way we parent our children has an impact on them, studies reveal that there is no direct correlation between a parenting style and the way a child turns out. In fact, it is not unusual for children brought up in the same household by the same set of parents following the same parenting style to turn out differently. How a particular child perceives a situation or a parenting style and responds to them can be diametrically opposite to the way their sibling reacts to the same situation. Therefore, it is impossible to find the best parenting style.

The question then is: what is the use of understanding the different parenting styles, identifying your own style and, for that matter, making an effort to tweak it?

The beauty of the parenting journey is that it is like an adventure, a long-distance hike, where you are unfamiliar with the route and the weather is unpredictable. You also don't know what all you will encounter, how you will react to the situations and what the final outcome will be. But the journey, with all its ups and downs, is fun and exciting; it is an emotional roller-coaster. The uncertainty only adds to the sense of fulfilment. Since we don't know what's at the next turn, the key to everything in the parenting journey is to remain conscious and be fully present in every situation. This approach will help you understand the situation and plan your actions accordingly. We are in the journey together with our children, each of us growing simultaneously in our own ways. Consider the fact that your child hasn't been this age before, and so she doesn't know how to handle it. Similarly, unless you've already been a parent, you too may not have brought up a child of this age before, and so you too do not have the expertise of managing this particular situation. While there is no one way of parenting, the idea is to adopt conscious parenting. And the first step to that is to know your parenting style.

Different Styles of Parenting

During the early 1960s, psychologist Diana Baumrind conducted a study on more than 100 preschool-age children.[*] Using naturalistic observation, parental interviews and other research methods, she identified some important dimensions of parenting. These dimensions include disciplinary strategies, warmth and nurturing, communication styles, and expectations of maturity and control.

Based on these dimensions, Baumrind suggested that the majority of parents display one of three different parenting styles: authoritarian, authoritative or permissive. Further research by E.E. Maccoby and J.A. Martin suggested adding a fourth parenting style to these original three. This fourth

---

[*]Baumrind, D. (1967). 'Child care practices anteceding three patterns of preschool behavior'. *Genetic Psychology Monographs*, 75(1), 43–88

style is called 'uninvolved'. Figure 1 depicts the four parenting styles and their approaches.

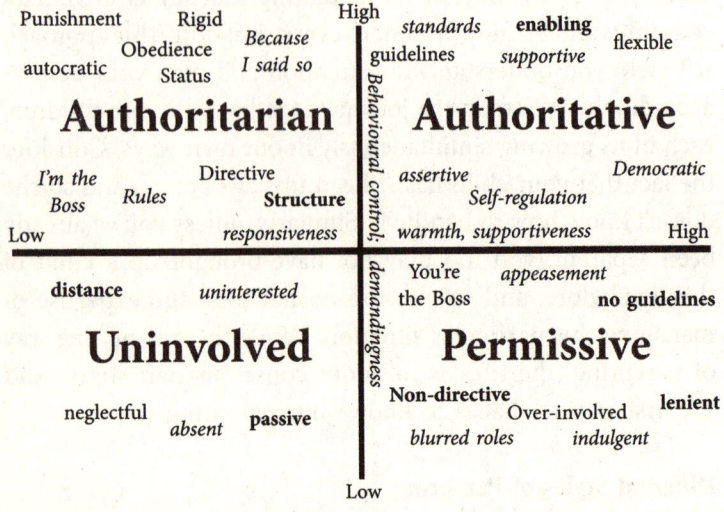

Figure 1. Parenting styles

As Figure 1 shows, the four parenting styles have been categorized based on the parameters of 'behavioural control' and 'warmth and supportiveness' between the parents and the children.

In the **authoritarian style**, the parents have control in their hands. Rules, regulations, punishments and behaviour are prescribed and managed by the parents. They expect the children to follow the rules without being told the reasoning behind said rules, 'because I say so'. In the **permissive style**, the parents are indulgent. The child is in charge and things are done as per the child's wishes. The parents are in appeasement mode and there are no guidelines for the children. Parents following the **authoritative style** believe in democracy. They set standards in consultation with children and believe in self-regulation. They have high expectations from their children, but also provide a warm and enabling environment. The **uninvolved style** is where parents are uninvolved and detached, and the child is neglected.

An individual may not fall in any one particular style of parenting. Some parents could have one dominant style, with the other styles too coming into play in different situations. It would be good for you to know your and your spouse's dominant styles. You can take our online survey[*] to find out your parenting style. If there are other family members at home who co-parent your child, they too should take the survey. This will help you understand your actions and responses, as well as those of others in the family.

At Parwarish, we propagate and recommend the **concerted parenting style**.[**] The name is derived from the word 'concert'.

Concert

noun

1. a musical performance given in public, typically by several performers or of several compositions.
2. FORMAL
   agreement or harmony.
   LAW
   joint action, especially in the committing of a crime
   transitive verb.
arrange (something) by mutual agreement or coordination.

---

*https://docs.google.com/forms/d/e/1FAIpQLSf76ILQ1ISYMqacqLwcIU3k
wDqtbxoJxdWbCkJ_k2rEmAMBrA/viewform
**https://www.youtube.com/watch?v=Wi7r4d9JFpY

The concerted parenting style is like conducting a concert together. Everyone is playing their respective instrument—from drums to flutes to guitars to percussion instruments—but what gets created is one song or one symphony. In this parenting style, the parents and children are performing a concert together as a family. Here, the parents are conscious of their dominant parenting style and they have the skill to use appropriate styles for every situation. Each member of the family, as well as the family as a whole, their actions and their communications, and the environment are all in harmony. It is this concerted style of parenting that this book aims to share with you.

The Parwarish Child Development Model

While we started researching on child-rearing and parenting in 2000, Parwarish was formally established in 2008. This book is based on our research of over two decades and our experience of working with parents and children for over a decade. Our mission has been of 'partnering and empowering parents, teachers and other caregivers in nurturing the nolimitness of every child'.

Over these years, we have worked extensively with parents of children as young as two years and as old as 28 years. The work we do with them is a combination of training and long-term coaching support, which has delivered extraordinary results for parents and children alike. The programme has managed to produce successful results with children across cultures, due to the child development model on which it is based. The fact that it takes into account our observations, analyses and interpretations of the actions and behaviours of children and adults drawn from our personal interactions with them, is what distinguishes the Parwarish child development model from those of yesteryears.

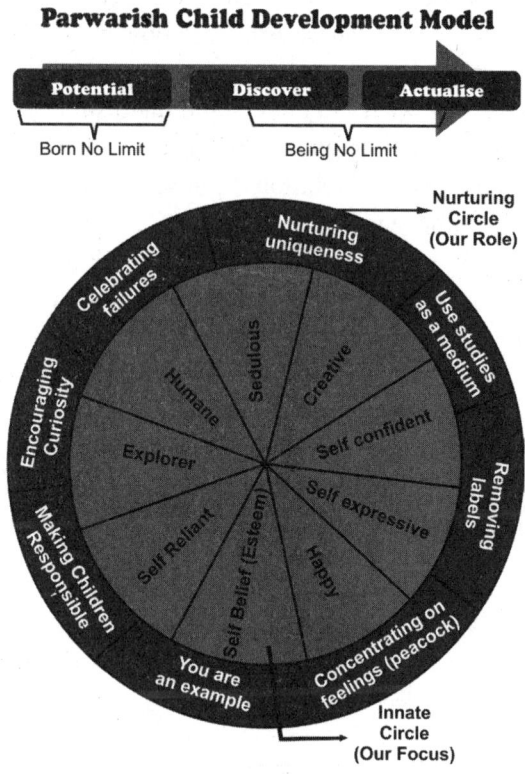

Figure 2. Parwarish Child Development Model[TM]

In this book, we will look at how you can use the model to achieve the following goals:

- Your child grows up to be a nolimit adult.
- You experience joy and fulfilment in day-to-day parenting.

Our tendency as humans is that when we consult another adult or an expert over a problem, we expect them to give us instant solutions. At Parwarish, we follow a slightly different approach. We listen to the problems that parents and children come to us with, we try to understand them, and we help them see things from a different perspective. We don't instruct; we help them discover the solutions themselves simply by opening them up to other viewpoints.

This book would disappoint anyone looking for quick-fix solutions or tips. We are talking about human beings here. A human being is a complex interplay of emotions, feelings, interpretations, knowledge, actions, reactions and responses. What's more, all these factors change by the moment. So, not only will something that works in one situation not necessarily work in another, something that works for one individual may not work for another in the same situation either—even if they are twins.

4

WHAT WE REALLY WANT
FOR OUR CHILDREN

One of my supervisors at a multinational company used to say that if you don't know where you want to go, you will never reach there—and even if you do, you won't realize it!

Even though it may sound clichéd, all journeys do begin with the end in mind. Have you ever asked for a ticket at a counter? Did you not ask for a ticket *to* a particular place? Without that information, the person on the other side would not be able to process your request. Similarly, the process of planning for a holiday or a trip starts with us deciding *where* we want to go; the rest of the planning—how we will travel, where we will stay, how many days it will take, how much money we will end up spending—follows.

Our parenting journey is, however, different. Here, more often than not, we don't start off knowing where we are going or what we really want—even though we may think otherwise. If we really ponder, we will realize we have never stopped to think about and articulate what we really want for our child. What normally happens is that one fine day, after around nine months of pregnancy, one becomes a parent. Suddenly there is this vulnerable life in your arms—a baby who cannot survive without your care. From day one, we jump into doing stuff—from feeding, changing, cleaning, and ensuring they are protected, to gradually helping them learn how to walk, talk, eat and then sending them off to school—taking care of their basic needs and ensuring that they are studying well, involved in some hobbies, learning some skills and so on.

But in the midst of all this, do you ever sit down alone or with your spouse to think and articulate, 'What do we really want for our child?' In my last 10 years of working with parents, I have not met even a handful who have done this consciously. We may be on the parenting journey for years without defining the purpose or the destination.

When Monica and I were expecting our first child, the question 'What do I really want for my child?' intrigued me. Did I want my child to be a doctor, an engineer, an artist, a teacher, a sportsperson or something else? But soon enough, I realized I was no one to decide this. This led to some other questions plaguing my mind. How do I figure out what the child would want to become? What would the world look like when this child grows up? Where would the child be—which part of the world? What opportunities would be available for the child? The list of questions was endless, but the fact was that neither did I have the right to plan this out for another individual—even if that individual was my own child—nor could I make a concrete plan, given the uncertainty of the future. How can one have a concrete vision for the future of a child yet to be born—a child whose abilities, preferences, likes and dislikes are yet unknown to us?

But wouldn't the absence of a vision mean that I would start off on the journey without knowing where to go? It was perhaps my training as an engineer and in management that led to me finding this absence of a goal disconcerting.

When I shared this with Monica, she was surprised—or rather perplexed at first. Why would we impose anything on our child? It would be their life and we as parents would simply be the support system. That was her line of thought— and she was bang on! And yet we kept talking about this paradox of setting off on a critical journey of our lives without a destination in mind. It seemed I was adamant about finding a logical reason for giving up on the need to have a destination to our parenting journey—even if it meant creating one. This fixation was ultimately a huge revelation—it was the beginning of the transformation of parenting for Monica and me.

The discussion between Monica and me that had started from my need to have a clear goal/destination in mind led us to an alternative question, which was more fundamental than the previous one. In this scenario of uncertainty, with us having no idea of what our child would be like and what their likes, dislikes and desires would be, which part of the world their life would take them to, what resources they would have access to and so on, what did we want for our child? We realized that we wanted our child to:

- Be happy
- Be fulfilled and contented
- Be independent
- Be self-reliant
- Be responsible for their life—their environment, their family, their health, etc.
- Be healthy
  - Physically
  - Mentally

- o Emotionally
- o Spiritually
- o Socially
- Be free from stress and anxiety (Is that possible in the real world? What's wrong in wishing for it, or even aiming for it?)
- Be courageous/fearless
- Be confident
- Be high on self-esteem
- Be inquisitive, be a learner
- Be tenacious to get up every time they fall
- Be part of—and contribute to—great relationships
- Be good at communicating
- Be a good human being
  - o Honest
  - o Truthful to self and others
  - o Respectful
  - o Caring and loving

The list was finally ready. The beauty of the list was that, irrespective of what our child would want to be or do in their life, if they possessed the above qualities and skills, we knew they would have a great life—and we would have done a great job as parents.

The next thought after creating this list was the apparent 'impossibility' of achieving it. It was like asking for the moon and hoping to actually get it. When we looked around us, we couldn't find someone with all of these qualities. Did these qualities exist? The answer was 'yes', but for one person to have them all was utopian. But over the years, during the course of our own parenting journey as well as that of the thousands of parents we have worked with, we have realized that achieving this list may be difficult, but it is definitely not impossible.

What the exercise gave us was a target, a goal for our child. The next step was to answer the following questions:

- What were we going to do?
- How were we going to achieve this?
- How would the two of us work together with our differences of opinions?
- How would we work together with the grandparents and the teachers?

While we didn't have the answers to these questions, we felt it was a battle half won, since Monica and I were completely aligned when it came to the goal we had in mind for our child.

Over the last 10 years, we have asked thousands of parents whom we have worked with at Parwarish the same question: in this world where the future is uncertain, what do you really want for your child? And their answers have been similar, if not the same. Whether the parent belongs to the Bheel tribe or is an urban industrialist, whether the parent is from India or from the West, they want the same things for their children.

When Vikram[*] and Sonam first came to us, they had been married for almost 20 years. Their sons Siddharth and Raghav were 16 and 13 years old respectively. In the first meeting, Sonam complained that Siddharth had become very rude and self-centred. We could hear the pain and disgust in her voice as she narrated how Siddharth would respond to her. She told us that she had to follow up on everything—from waking him up in the morning for school, to keeping his clothes in the wardrobe, to keeping his books and other stuff

---

[*]Real names have been withheld to maintain client confidentiality.

in place—even getting him to eat at the table with the family. The list was endless.

Sonam was exasperated with the amount of following up she had to do the whole day. She was concerned that Siddharth would be on his own at college in a year's time, and he needed to start taking responsibility of himself and learn to manage things on his own. There were times when her exasperation had led to her shouting at him to complete his work. Siddharth would then shout back. He would tell her that she was being difficult, and her pestering him was the reason for his unhappiness and bad moods, which in turn led to bad performance at school.

Vikram would take his son's side and be critical of Sonam's temper and her unnecessary follow-ups. According to him, Sonam's behaviour was affecting the peace, harmony and happiness at home. Vikram felt that with Siddharth about to leave for college in a year's time, they should avoid unpleasant conversations at home. His philosophy was to ensure that Siddharth had a good time in this 'last' year at home before he ventured out for college and then his career, so that he could have fond memories of the time spent at home. According to Vikram, Sonam had been focusing on petty stuff, which was adversely affecting the mood of everyone at home.

In the first meeting itself it became very clear that the role apportioned to the mother—of taking care of things at home—was becoming difficult for Sonam, and with Vikram too holding her responsible for the unhappiness building up in their home, she was feeling wronged. Sonam was feeling that her efforts over many years had not been acknowledged, and with Vikram supporting Siddharth's viewpoint, she felt cornered and alone.

The frequent altercations between Siddharth and Sonam were getting louder and harsher with time, and the equations were getting bitter. Of late, Vikram and Raghav had also started getting involved in these altercations, resulting in a hostile environment building up at home.

In our first meeting with the family, we asked the parents to articulate what they wanted for their kids. After a few minutes of facilitation, they shared that they wanted both Siddharth and Raghav to:

- Be happy
- Be self-dependent
- Take responsibility of their studies and health
- Be healthy
- Manage their screen time appropriately
- Be respectful to their parents and others
- Be confident
- Have great relationships
- Be good human beings
  - Honest
  - Caring and loving

We asked Vikram and Sonam to take the list with them and over the course of the following week, observe and note instances of their interaction with the children, and as a family, that they were oriented towards the goals they had listed—and those that weren't. When they met us a week later, we found that while the situation had not improved, both Vikram and Sonam had diligently done the exercise we had asked of them.

Sonam shared that she had asked Siddharth to stop using the laptop after he had been gaming for a couple of hours. She explained how her action was purely oriented towards helping him learn time management, so that long, uninterrupted hours of gaming didn't impact his performance in studies. She also shared that she had to 'counsel' Siddharth on why he needed to start taking greater ownership for his work and schedules. Siddharth, however, perceived Sonam's action as being autocratic and insensitive, which resulted in an argument between them. Vikram intervened during this altercation, asking Sonam to not be so stringent with timelines and giving Siddharth permission to play for longer. This led to yet another argument between Sonam and Vikram.

According to Sonam, Vikram's approach to resolving all disputes between mother and son by agreeing with the latter simply because he did not want the children to be unhappy was incorrect. Vikram, on the other hand, argued that forcing him to reduce his screen time would make Siddharth unhappy, and being in a bad mood would mean he wouldn't be able to study.

The parents got into a heated argument right in the middle of their session with us. After getting them to stop arguing, we dismantled the entire context behind their argument. What they saw in the next few minutes for themselves was:

- That they had their own views on achieving the list of 'what they wanted for Siddharth' in this episode.
- Vikram was concerned about the happy mood— pleasure, not happiness—of the child and for Sonam, ensuring discipline was more important. Neither of them was focusing on the list they had prepared.
- After a few minutes, 'I am right' became paramount and the discussion—which had turned into an argument— became all about each of them trying to prove that they were right. What they wanted for Siddharth—and indeed for both their children—had taken a backseat.

It was then that they suddenly realized that the focus of their argument had shifted from the child to proving each other wrong. They both decided that going forward, they would try to articulate their intentions to each other in their discussions, which would help them keep the discussions on track.

The list they had prepared in their first session with us was in the form of a chart, which they displayed on the wall next to the refrigerator at their home. A week later, they shared that they had also talked about the list with both their children, and to their surprise they found that both Siddharth and Raghav wanted the same for themselves. So, from being on two different sides negotiating—often aggressively—with each other, they started articulating the intentions behind their actions to each other and the understanding levels at home started to increase.

What follows is aimed at helping you acquire the tools with which you can make small but critical tweaks in your daily interactions and communications. Doing so will help you achieve the goals that you list for your children. The list may seem impossible, but it isn't. The journey that you are on with this book will debunk many myths—and the list being utopian is one such myth!

ACTION HACK

- 'What do we really want for our child?' Co-create with your spouse or partner a list that answers this question for you as a parent.
- Involve your child(ren) in the making of this list.
- Involve your spouse/parents/parents-in-law or any other adult who plays a significant role in your child's life in this exercise.

BONUS

Display this list prominently at your home. This will give you a simple way to keep the list alive and present in your consciousness. Also ask your children what they want for themselves. Support them in getting to the 'why' behind what they want. You will be pleasantly surprised with the list they end up making.

5

OUR ROLE AS PARENTS

What is your role as a parent? Before we try to answer this question, it is important to recognize that *becoming* a parent and *being* a parent are two different things. Having a child—whether biological or by way of adoption or surrogacy—is just the beginning of a long journey. The parenting journey is like a roller-coaster, but if we look at it another way, parenting is a way of creating the future—our future, the future of our children, the future of society, the future of this planet.

As a parent you contribute to a life, first creating a space for the child to know their potential and then helping them actualize that potential. The first step, therefore, is to consciously think of an empowering answer to the question, 'what is your role as a parent?' Take a few minutes off before reading further and dwell on this question. Become aware of the various facets of parenting and articulate what being a parent means.

- Being a role model
  - Nurturing qualities like love, compassion, honesty
  - Inculcating good habits and respect for self and others
  - Encouraging healthy eating habits
  - Building a value system

- Being their confidant
  - Providing them with emotional support
  - Being there for them when they need you
  - Accepting them for what they are
  - Listening to them
  - Understanding them
  - Providing them the space to talk and share
  - Communicating with them
  - Sharing with them
  - Playing with them
- Being their guide
  - As they set goals in their life
  - As they take responsibility for their studies, health, hygiene, screen time, etc.
  - Guiding them, pushing them, helping them gain experiences and exposure
  - Motivating and encouraging them
  - Coaching them
  - Letting them take their own decisions
  - Providing them with necessary resources like food, clothes, schooling, etc.

The fundamental idea behind articulating this is to really be present as you define for yourself your role as a parent. Being present in the experience and using the tools that this book provides will help you have a fulfilling parenting experience.

ACTION HACK

Prepare this list with your spouse. Look at all you need to do and evaluate your current actions.

Role of a Father

Parenting has traditionally been considered a mother's job. But it certainly isn't just that—and I promise every father that they will love me for this part of the book. A whole new world is waiting for you—a world of joy and fulfilment, which will be worth every minute of your life. Being an active participant in parenting a child helps in nurturing the parents'—both mother's and father's—managerial skills, which can be brought into use to excel at work. Yes, you heard me right. Parenting can help boost your career as a manager, because it makes you more aware of another individual's existence, while also teaching you how to influence their behaviour—skills that can help you manage teams at work.

Traditionally, the role assigned to the father has been that of a provider, and women are seen as nurturers—tuned by nature to take care of and provide comfort to the child. Even in the twenty-first century, the major onus of parenting is assigned primarily to the mother. Sure, the nine-month pregnancy period, when the child is an inseparable part of the mother 24x7, gives her a headstart. Perhaps the level of attachment is also greater for a mother. But to assign the parenting role exclusively to one gender wouldn't be correct.

Let's look at this idea of both parents being involved in the process of parenting from a different perspective.

In general, we, as a society at large, have separated gender roles and traits in our language, our understanding and our day-to-day social interactions. These three are distinct fields, and the separation has led to us and our children neither accessing nor experiencing nor utilizing the entire range of emotions and capabilities available to a human being.

I see the role of the father as a critical contribution towards that. Some of the masculine and feminine traits are listed below. This is not an exhaustive list, but will give you a sense of what I am talking about.

Masculine Traits	Feminine Traits
Focus on own needs	Compassionate care for others
Competitive	Collaborative
Assertive	Receptive, grateful
Protect	Nurture
Goal-directed	Relationship-directed
Rational, linear and logical thinking	Intuitive
Independence	Interdependence
Mono-task	Multitask
Bias for action	Patience, forgiveness
Spatial	Temporal

The masculine and feminine traits have nothing to do with the sex of an individual. Any individual can exhibit any of these traits. However, we tend to misread the masculine traits as those present only in men and the feminine traits as exhibited only by women—we tend to put them into separate boxes. What's worse is that when, say, a man shows compassion and nurturing behaviour, he is called feminine, or even considered 'not man enough'. Similarly, an assertive, goal-oriented and competitive woman is considered aggressive—with the word having a predominantly negative connotation in her context.

Ideally, a balanced individual would have traits from both sets—in fact, that would help an individual fully experience life. However, conventionally, those entrusted with moulding us, along with the society at large, tend to nurture the masculine traits in men and the feminine traits in women—to the point where these become 'natural'.

How can we ensure that our child acquires a balanced composition of the two sets of traits—masculine and feminine? By involving both parents in the parenting process. Children often copy what the parents do. Therefore, the involvement of both parents in the process of parenting exposes the child to a wide range of actions and traits from both sets. When a father depicts the feminine traits of, say, being involved in the process of nurturing the child, patience, good listening skills and empathy, a male child will imbibe them. Similarly, the father's involvement in bringing up a girl child naturally transfers goal-orientation, the idea of being a provider and of having a competitive spirit to the girl. This is not to say that a child cannot learn goal-orientation from the mother—the child can pick this up from either parent, but in a family with traditional roles allocated to men and women, the child is likely to pick this up from the father.

So, I would urge the fathers—or soon-to-be fathers—reading this book to spend time with their children. The father, as much as the mother, has a lead role in the child's life. Don't restrict yourself to playing only a supportive role! Your involvement—or lack thereof—determines your child's access to all the traits available for a human being.

ACTION HACK

- Assess the qualities and traits that you can currently observe in your child.
- Assess the prominent traits that you see in yourself and your spouse.
- Think of the traits your child can pick up from both of you.
- List down the traits that you think have got suppressed for them, and the ones that you are not able to express freely. This will lead you to a list of traits to focus on for yourself and your child in future.

6

BEING A LIFELONG LEARNER

The year is 1990. 'Parents' constitute of 'Mother' and 'Father'. Three decades later, we are in 2020, and a set of parents now comprises of Mother, Father and Media. The world has changed and the media is not just the third parent, but also the medium through which virtually everyone is parenting children. Movies, TV serials, advertisements, cartoons, etc. were means of entertainment earlier. Today, they have become influencers in your child's life. Advertisers, realizing that it is easier to influence a child than a more rationally thinking adult and also seeing how children are often at the centre of decision-making in the current family structure, have started reorienting their campaigns. Whether they are selling children's products or something else, they now target the child of the house.

Children are like sponge, always absorbing things from their environment, be it language, behaviour, relationships, morality, religion, values and preferences: what to buy, what to wear, what to eat, what to play and so on. As parents, we may not like it, we may not approve of it, we may even hate it, but the truth is that media—TV, mobiles, social media, Netflix, etc.—has invaded our homes and is not so covertly parenting our children. In many cases, it may well be the parent that spends the most amount of time with the child!

So, let's make a start today. The first step is to accept the power of media and make the shift from 'parenting vs. media' to 'parenting and media'. Media/technology is great; so, let's embrace it and look at ways and means to leverage it rather than fight it.

If we look around us, we will find that the world has changed rapidly and dramatically in the last 30 years. For instance,

- We now have access to more and better facilities.
- The parameters of success have undergone a significant change.
- Technology is changing by the minute.
- Knowledge is freely available.
- Morality has undergone drastic shifts.

And the list goes on. Another significant change that we have been witness to over the last few years is the increase in stress levels:

- Health issues—physical, mental, emotional and social— are growing all over.
- Suicide rates, psychological disorders, drug addiction, alcoholism and other social issues are increasing at an alarming rate.
- Family values, respect, morality, safety, etc. are taking a plunge.
- Competition is replacing cooperation.

With these shifts in the various elements that constitute our environment, what worked three decades ago will not work any longer. As parents, we need to be conscious of the shifts in the environment and adapt to them. While parenting is considered a natural skill for parents, we must accept that we need to unlearn and relearn some things with the changing times. It is similar to how an expert at driving in India would need to acquire new skills when in the US because of the use of left-hand driving there and different (and more rigorous) traffic rules.

While we may be theoretically aware of the differences between the driving patterns and rules between the two countries, it would be another thing altogether to be able to drive in such a situation. For parenting too, new contexts, new methods and new skills need to acquired, learnt and practised.

So, how do we make the shift when it comes to parenting? A few starting points could be:

- It is a competitive world out there, and the children too are under stress to perform. Merely being a provider won't work anymore; learn to be a good listener to your child. A critical aspect of parenting now is being a sounding board for your child. The first step to entering their world is to know it.
- Technology is part and parcel of our everyday lives. Cell phones have become extensions of our bodies! We carry them everywhere. It is important to accept that we cannot fight technology—so we must embrace it instead. It is possible that we are not conversant with all of its functionalities, but the way forward is to learn.
- The most important skill is to be open to learning. E-mail, internet, e-commerce and social media platforms such as Facebook and Instagram make information readily available to us and allow us to share things. We cannot deny the fact that technology

has brought convenience to our lives. So, let's leverage technology. A few ways to do so would be:

- o Learn e-mailing. Schools are shifting to sending updates and homework on mails.
- o Try and be comfortable with e-commerce—buying and selling online.
- o Open up to the internet, which has opened up the world for us. Knowledge is available many times over on the internet.
- o Read books, magazines, dailies, weeklies, etc. to keep up-to-date with what is happening around us. It brings us in touch with the current world—the world of our children.

The fact is that while we all know the importance of keeping ourselves in sync with the present times, most of us still don't take the first step. Let's go over a few barriers we face, so that we can be conscious of them and prepare ourselves to overcome them:

- 'Learning' is a word that reminds us of our school days and of four things in particular—subjects, tests, exams and results.
- The thought '*ab iss umar mein kya seekheingey*? (What will I learn at this age?)'
- There are enough issues in our life already and I don't want to add one more.

Whenever thoughts such as these come to your mind, remember those school days—even when learning was difficult and stressful, it was the most enjoyable time of our lives. Learning and enjoyment are two sides of the same coin. Put half an hour of 'learning' in your daily schedule; it's easier than it sounds. There are enough avenues available; for example,

- The internet has all the content. Google your questions and you will get enough videos and learning material.
- Bookstalls are full of self-help books. They aren't half as bad as some people think!
- Ask your child to teach you. They would make great tutors, and they learn while teaching. This also surreptitiously keeps them away from the things you want them to be away from!
- Contact your child's school. They would be keen to support you.
- Ask the experts!

So, let's begin today! Let's walk this road of learning with our children. It's a great path to tread and partner with them on.

ACTION HACK

There are skills, knowledge and qualities that you want to acquire for yourself. Hobbies and activities which you used to love doing in your childhood and teenage—take them up! Get back to reading, walking, playing, etc. Let's make a start today.

7

BUSTING THE MYTH OF
THE GENERATION GAP

It was one of those rare Sunday afternoons when I could relax with my family. Raj, a friend of mine, called. He sounded furious. He started off by telling me that he found it impossible to get his son Rohan to follow what he would say.

Rohan was 12 years old, and there was constant debate between the father and the son. The father didn't want his son to watch a particular television series which according to him wasn't age-appropriate, but the son would just not listen. Raj had tried virtually everything to get Rohan to understand that he didn't find the language and theme of the series appropriate for Rohan's age. What began as Raj's attempt to explain led to him shouting at Rohan, and finally taking away Rohan's privileges; yet, none of it seemed to work. Raj was finally compelled to put restrictions on Rohan's access to the DTH connection, eventually going for a complete disconnect.

The absence of a DTH connection, however, impacted other members of the family. Rohan's grandparents had to miss out on their share of television. Raj's wife was upset with both Rohan and him, for she felt that the others were getting impacted simply because the father and son couldn't resolve their conflict. What had started as an altercation over cable television then spread in scope to other areas as well—Raj and Rohan started arguing over the latter's wake-up time on school days; Raj also didn't agree with Rohan's choice of hairstyle and his reading habits. Soon, Rohan started to distance himself from Raj.

There is every chance that most of us have been part of such a situation, either as a parent or with our own parents when we were young. Such altercations are the supposed outcome of what is called the generation gap. The *Cambridge Dictionary* defines 'generation gap' as 'a situation in which older and younger people do not understand each other because of their different experiences, opinions, habits, and behaviour'. Essentially, children, as they grow up, believe that their parents don't understand them and their world. Similarly, parents believe that by the time their children are teenagers, they no longer understand the world of the parents. The differences in these two worlds with respect to language, moral and ethical standards, ease of use when it comes to technology, media, work attitudes and so on are too great. The progress and development in various societies and the influence of various cultures add to this gap.

If you consider these factors, you will realize that the reasons for the generation gap are external and constantly changing. Not only that, the speed of change is itself changing exponentially. This rate of change and resultant societal shifts were very slow in the 1950s. The pace has increased over the decades and is likely to only increase further. In the 1950s, a generation gap would occur over a period of 20 years; today, you can sense a generation gap even between two individuals who are just a couple of years apart in age.

Will this reality of change ensure that the gap between parents and their children keeps widening? That's externalizing a critical element of our lives and being at the receiving end of the issue.

Let's examine this gap in understanding other people and see how it can apply to the gap between parents and their children.

There is a great chance of you and your spouse belonging, more or less, to the same generation. There can, of course, be exceptions, but here we will focus on a scenario where both partners are from the same generation. Have you noticed that despite this, a given situation can evoke very different emotions and reactions from the two of you? Actually, most of our altercations and fights originate from the fact that we understand, feel and respond to situations very differently. Some of us may have spent years making our spouse think like us and understand the intensity of a situation the way we do, or we may have absorbed our spouse's way of thinking and reacting.

Here, I have a simple question for you. Does your spouse like to eat the same thing you do, have the same hobbies and interests, or is left with the same feeling as you after an incident? The answer is no. They are another individual, with a mind and a heart of their own, their own way of thinking and feeling. In other words, a particular situation would more often than not fail to elicit the exact same feelings and thoughts as us in our spouses—or any other individual, for that matter. So, what do we need to do to understand how another individual feels and thinks? Simply ask them—ask them to get to know their world, from a space of inquiry and not from one of judgment or evaluation; not to assess whether they are wrong or right or to make them understand your perspective, but to simply understand a space that we don't know.

The idea is not to bridge the gap with an individual with a different way of thinking, feeling or responding—the key lies in knowing and acknowledging the difference. We must realize it isn't a gap, but simply a difference that we need to acknowledge and appreciate. The world is changing and changing fast. The way out is to build communication to a level where we can understand and acknowledge each other's differences.

Let us now extrapolate this differences between people belonging to the same generation to those across generations.

In this ever-changing world, our children's exposure to everything—schools, books, media, food, travel, relationships, sports, hobbies and so on—is very different from our own. This is the reason why our responses to the common elements that have changed over time differ.

As parents, Monica and I wished to avoid the 'generation gap' with our children. We started working towards it right when both our children were quite young. We made an effort to try to understand their world, to know the happenings at school and in their lives generally, to understand how things impacted them and what they thought and felt about what was happening around them. Also, we ensured that we shared with them things that were happening in our world—our workplace, projects we were working on, relationships at work and in the family, our feelings and thoughts about how our lives were moving and how everything was impacting us. This sounds easier said than done—and this two-way communication, simply with the intention of sharing and understanding each other, is a continuous and never-ending journey.

Our lives are amalgamations of a lot of ups and downs. As we grow older, our lives seem to become more complicated. As children, the travails of life hadn't hit most of us. All we had to take care of was our studies, hobbies and some sports. Earning a living, managing a boss, peers and the team at work, the targets, the appraisals, the business cycles; maintaining a fine balance in our relationships, be it with parents, in-laws and extended family or with the spouse and children; along with keeping track of societal norms—all this together makes for a tough and complicated life as an adult.

As parents, we often think of how our children, when they grow up, would have to deal with all this, and so we don't want to burden them with the nitty-gritties of adult life while they are still so young. Or we may wonder how to tell them that we are struggling or making mistakes—and thus break the myth that adults have their lives sorted out! The common lines of thought that keep us away from sharing our lives with our children are:

- They are too young to burden them with serious stuff.
- They won't understand.
- It will lead to more questions and I may not have the answers.
- What will they start thinking about me?
- What opinions would they form about others in the family?
- It's their age to have fun and enjoy life; there's no point bringing up other issues.

I gave up a high-paying job with a multinational company to start Parwarish, a dream venture set up solely with the vision to make a difference. There was no business model behind it, nor a monetization plan. This shift was one of the most difficult decisions of my life. In the last ten years, this has been an arduous journey, starting from enrolling people to join Parwarish and training them, designing programmes and conducting them, to approaching educational institutes and parents to ask them to come and learn this art. There have been times when we were exasperated, when we argued and struggled to meet the organizational expenses.

One thing that has worked for me as a person and a father is the courage to share my journey the way I am experiencing it with my children. Even Vaanya, my younger child, who is now 12 years old, has been my confidant for the last four or five years. We have a daily routine of a 15–30 minute evening walk, where we also run errands. I use this time to share my day and feelings with my daughter. There have been times when I have had an altercation at work and it left a negative impact on both me and the colleague involved. I would gather the courage to tell Vaanya about it. One day a few years ago, when I had a big argument with a colleague to whom even Vaanya is very close, my first thought was to not share it with her, lest she may start judging my colleague, which would then create a distance between them. Moreover, I was feeling guilty of my own behaviour and I feared that she may judge me for my inappropriate response in the disagreement with my colleague. As we walked together that evening, perhaps noticing that I was very quiet, she stretched to put her hand on my shoulders.

'Dad, how's life?' she asked. The question shook me out of my thoughts. I didn't want to lie to her and yet I was finding it difficult to share my thoughts. I had shared so much with her earlier—about financial struggles and even my altercations with my wife Monica—but somehow this felt harder.

The question I asked myself was: do I want her to start thinking about what she should or shouldn't tell me—should she too pause and think if there was something that she should hide from me? The answer to this was definitely in the negative. I always want to be the person whom she can rely on to share anything with no inhibitions. I want to be the space that she can take for granted. I would always be there for her, no matter what. With these thoughts, it now became clear to me what my own choice should be.

I began telling her how I wanted to do a certain programme my way and how my colleague was adamant that it wasn't the most efficient way. We had both lost our cool, shouted at each other and ended the discussion without any conclusion. I also shared that I was worried that it would spoil her relationship with my teammate. She patiently heard me out, patted me on my shoulder and said: 'Dad, it's not good to bottle up your feelings. You can share things with me anytime. We are buddies!'

It was great to just listen to her say this. What a beautiful moment it was to know that my nine-year-old daughter thought of us as buddies! With Monica travelling a lot for her work, I didn't have to wait for her to return home to share the everyday things—I had Vaanya, who would listen to me without judgment. As I shared my life with Vaanya, including my difficulties and my 'imperfect side', what developed between us was a deeper connection. In the process, a dialogue was created which made her realize that:

- It is fine to have these emotions.
- It is okay to be upset.
- A father and daughter *can* share things.

- Her father is not perfect and he has his shortcomings.

The evening walks have become a great source of energy and connection between us. On days when we are not able to have these chats, we feel there is something missing from our day. The communication between us is two-way. Just as I share things with her, she too pours out everything to me—her daily life and encounters with friends and other people. If she is upset with a friend, she tells me. It has been quite a journey—from being a father who felt vulnerable sharing his life as it is, to reaching that point in the parent–child bond where I can share the happenings of my life with both my children, without filtering anything out—unlike what we parents normally do: hide our difficulties from our children, thinking that they will get impacted, while also getting into advising them on what to do and what not to when they share their travails and feelings. Sometimes, we camouflage our difficult times as 'learning' in our conversation. These are not the times to teach, advise, create learning. These are times of pure, unadulterated, unhindered sharing, where we are unmasking the 'perfect' parent and taking about the human (imperfect) side of ours.[*]

In order to develop this constant two-way communication with our children, where we set an example for them to not feel the need to filter anything out when it comes to sharing updates on their lives with us, the first step is to notice the thoughts that stop us from sharing our lives with them. As you go through the following list, also try to read in these points the parallel arguments that your child may think of against sharing their ups and down with you.

---

[*]https://www.youtube.com/watch?v=aI2pbveINJ0

- They are too young to be burdened with serious stuff. (Parents are already doing a lot, and they are going through a lot of stuff themselves. Why should I burden them with my stuff?)
- They won't understand.
- It will lead to more questions and I may not have the answers.
- What will they think about me?
- What opinions would they form about others in the family? (What opinions would they form about my friends?)
- It's their age to have fun and enjoy life and so there's no point bringing up other issues. (They have already done enough for me. I don't want them to get upset. Let them be at peace.)

We wouldn't want such thoughts to hold them back—so we shouldn't hold back ourselves either.

In our home, topics like these make for dinner-time conversations. We talk to each other about the happenings of the day and the emotions the various events roused in us. We follow one rule: there will be no advising or commenting on whatever the other person shared. The only aim of this exercise is to know the world of the other person.

The generation difference is a fact, but it is up to us to not let that difference become a gap. All we need to do can be summed up in two steps. One, 'I don't know what it is to be them, let me ask' and two, 'They don't know what it is to be us. Let me tell them.'

8

UNDERSTANDING YOUR CHILD'S WORLD

It sometimes seems impossible to understand our own children's behaviour—especially after they hit their teenage years, when they suddenly become unpredictable, uncouth, unreliable, lazy, rebellious, aggressive and so on, even though they may have behaved 'normally' till then. We are all told that our children's teenage years would be the most difficult for us to manage as parents, and yet the reality seems even more daunting than those prior warnings implied.

Let's look at how teenagers mostly appear to us:

- Ruthless.
- Aggressive.
- Forcing their way with adults.
- Not willing to fall in line—they want everything their way.
- Listening to instructions is almost impossible—they have to argue and need justifications for everything we ask of them.
- Their music tastes, dressing sense, daily schedules, food preferences, lingo, etc. just don't match with ours or don't even fit in our definition of normal.
- Bingeing is the new normal—whether it is on food, drinks, games, time with friends, movies, shows! Every

indulgence is in extremes; asking a teenager to do anything in moderation is asking for the moon.

- Mostly on a short fuse, little things elicit extreme reactions—something can trigger a loud expression of displeasure while at other times, you may find them withdrawing into their shell.
- Experimenting, without any fear of things going wrong. They seem to ignore the potential dangers to health or well-being when trying new things and experiences. It seems like they are always on a dare!
- Manipulating and negotiating come naturally to them at this age. As a parent, the negotiations can be so exasperating that sometimes you just want to give in.

At this point, let us not assign any negative connotations to any of the aspects mentioned in the list. Let's first look at the picture from the adolescents' point of view.

We will not rely on a hypothetical discussion to understand the adolescents' perspective. Instead, let us take a short journey back to our own adolescence. I am sure a lot of you would say that we were not like this, that we were far easier to handle, that our parents didn't have to deal with the teenagers of this century and definitely not with the kind of exposure these kids have. But instead of indulging in any kind of comparison or trying to defend our side of the story, let us focus on empathizing with the adolescents of today. Let us do a small exercise.

Sit in the most comfortable position you can. Try not to cross your arms or legs. Leave all the thoughts running and playing in your mind. Be present in this room. Be with yourself. Take a deep breath and, as you exhale, allow your body to relax. Let your scalp and forehead and your face relax.

Let your tongue and your throat and your shoulders relax. Let your back and your abdomen and your pelvis relax. Let your breathing fall into a rhythm as you relax your legs and feet. Now, take yourself to the time when you were 14/15 years old. Think of yourself standing in front of a mirror. Now think of the following questions as that 14/15-year-old.

- How do you look? How tall or short are you?
- Look at your hair. Do you keep it long or short? How do you style your hair?
- What is the complexion of your skin?
- Do you have hair on your arms and legs?
- Have you started growing facial hair—beard and moustache?
- Can you feel a little huskiness in your voice or has it not changed yet?
- What is the size of your breasts?
- What is the length of your skirt?
- Do your periods impact you physically and emotionally?
- Are you conscious of your growing and ever-changing body?
- Are you conscious of boys/girls staring at you?
- Are you worried about your height? Do you compare yourself with others?
- Do you find yourself curious about 'sex' and the opposite gender? Where did you first learn about sex or related things?
- Do you wonder if you are popular among girls/boys?
- Do you want to be a part of the happening group of children who hang out together in school or elsewhere?
- What are you saying to yourself about yourself? Do

you feel good about yourself or do you constantly feel like you are not good enough?

- What do you look forward to in school?
- Imagine yourself attending your favourite teacher's class. How do you feel? What is your attention level? Do you enjoy that class?
- How does your body react when the teacher you don't like is about to arrive? Do you like the subject they teach? How do you feel around exam time—from the preparations to the results? Think back to a time when you got great marks, and also a time when you scored lower than your expectations.
- Take a look at your mood throughout the day. How was it? Were you generally happy? Angry? Irritated? When you came back home and your parents asked you about school, were you able to tell them how you truly felt?
- Is there someone you can talk your heart out to? Is there someone you are attracted to? Can you talk openly about it with your friends/parents/teachers? Are you satisfied with your social circle or do you constantly feel alone?

Be with this adolescent you are imagining right now. Be in this world. Be with this feeling.

You will realize that you had your own unique journey through those years. There is nothing to justify, nothing to compare between your children and your own times. Going back in time to when you were 14/15 years old and responding to these questions will remind you of the roller-coaster that those teenage years were. Now, examine and experience the following:

- The travails you experienced with respect to your ever-changing body, your insecurities and anxieties around sexuality, relationships with family members, relationships with friends and the opposite gender.
- How difficult and irritating it was with everyone around asking what you want to do in your life—the subject choices, the career choices and so on.
- Parents saying you were 'grown-up enough to handle stuff' and the very next moment saying 'you are not old enough to understand some stuff'. Wasn't it really confusing? Didn't it seem like they were using the 'child'/'grown-up' tag as per their convenience?
- Parents and teachers would often tell you to not do the very things that your friends were asking you to do. Parents would tell you to share everything, while your friends advised against sharing everything with parents.

The teenage years are all about physical, mental and emotional changes, increasing academic pressure, the constant dilemma between what is right and what is not, adults accusing us of spending too much time with friends, and the time when we start getting sexually attracted. Some of us sail through the years while others have a difficult time.

Looking back at my own teenage years, I would describe them as being not too much of a roller-coaster. My life was quite simple and safe, and my day revolved around school, home and the playground right in front of our house. I was an average student who would score around 60 per cent marks (while in today's super-competitive times, this score would raise red flags, back in the 1970s/80s it wasn't alarming). A quiet student, my participation level in class was just enough to survive.

I had two close friends, with whom I would sit during classes and share food during the lunch break. There were two warring groups in the class and the three of us were not part of either. My primary reason for not getting into either group was the fear of being caught and beaten up by the other.

My interactions with girls were non-existent—I would get tongue-tied in front of them, as if it was wrong to talk to them. Once back from school, my day revolved around cricket. I would spend some time eating my lunch and completing my homework—which seemed like a waste of time—and then I would rush to the playground to play cricket till it was too dark for us to see the ball. Social occasions were limited to family functions and get-togethers, where I would hang out and chat with my two cousins.

It may sound odd in today's times when children become aware of sex and sexuality at a very early age, but these remained a mystery to me till a younger cousin told me about them! I would find my classmates giggling away at the chapter on the reproduction system, but I had no idea why it elicited that reaction and all the whispering. I never had the courage to ask them why, and I would join them in the giggling to save myself from embarrassment.

While life wasn't too complicated for me, my friends would talk of and share the difficulties they were facing—the confusions they had about their bodies, issues with girlfriends and the fights they had with their parents.

While my teenage years weren't too eventful, there were times when I felt anxious and scared. I had a few questions that bothered me, but I could never gather the courage to talk to my parents about them. In fact, I never had anyone with whom I could share my thoughts about school and classes, my questions about my body, my confusion about the career path I should pursue, the bullying I faced and the fear I had of being picked on at school, the feeling I had of being a weakling (as I was one of the shortest and leanest students in the class) and so on. At times, it felt as if something was wrong with me, or that my understanding of life and its issues was inadequate, which made me anxious.

And then I would find around me some people whom I envied for their confidence and ability to speak up—but perhaps I even had a bit of contempt for their recklessness. There were times when I would catch myself saying 'I wish I had guts like them'; at other times, I would find them self-centred and would not want to be like them.

My friend Vikas could easily interact with girls in the class, and he always had a lot of stories to share about his escapades outside of school. I used to hate his guts—and sometimes, him. At times, he seemed to be having a great time, and yet sometimes, as if he was struggling. Being a disruption in the class and pulling a fast one on the teachers were his forte. Teasing the girls of the class during their menstrual cycle was normal for him. They would hate him for this and always try to avoid him. Whenever the teachers asked him about which stream he would choose later in his studies, he would be completely non-committal. He would simply say that it would depend on the marks he scored.

When I met him a couple of years ago, after a gap of 30 years, he had a retail setup in a local market. We chatted over coffee one day. We started reminiscing about the school days. He started off in his usual style of boasting about his guts—the run-ins with school authorities, how he managed to squeeze out of difficult situations, his escapades with girls, the fights he had in his locality and so on. Gradually, he shared what he was undergoing then. He told me he felt very lonely in that phase—he felt that no one understood him and he had no emotional support. The things he did seemed very exciting and got him everyone's attention. People would criticize his behaviour, but no one understood the reasons behind it. He shared how he felt that he lacked in his life the presence of someone who would listen to him and empathize with him before giving him advice.

That conversation made me see something I had never noticed before. I had been envious of his confidence and sometimes held him responsible for disruptions in class. As someone of the same age, dealing with the same kind of adolescence development, I could never understand that both of us were being impacted by hormonal changes. That tumultuous phase had shaped our lives—Vikas was still haunted by the actions of his teenage years. We sought the same thing—an adult figure in whom we could confide without the fear of judgement; someone who would listen to us, empathize with us and guide us. However, such an adult figure was often lacking in our lives—and is often missing from the lives of all teenagers, barring a few fortunate ones.

When we started talking about our children, Vikas shared that he was unable to be that supportive adult figure for his own 14-year-old daughter Tanvi, who was going through similar spaces, and any effort to get into her world would lead to a heated discussion between them. The endeavour to get closer to her and assume a more supportive role was in fact pushing her away.

Before getting into how we can dismantle this paradox, let's first look at what the world of an adolescent looks like in 2019. Thirty years since my own time, there is definitely a lot more chaos to handle. What our children are currently going through is a few hundred times more overwhelming than what we experienced. Greater exposure to media and the internet has opened their world to sex, alcohol, drugs and violent video games at a much younger age. Gadgets, mobile phones and laptops have invaded their everyday lives like never before. Add to this the easily available and innumerable options of unhealthy (junk) food. And then there is the weight of expectations—for them to excel at everything, from academics to sports to other hobbies!

The teenagers of today are exposed to cultures from across the world. They need to deal with comparisons at a much higher level: what school they go to, where they celebrate their birthdays, which car their parents own, where they go for their holidays, the clothing and accessories brands they wear, where their family lives and dines—the list is endless.

Today, there is immense performance pressure. In our times, parents didn't bother too much about our academic scores, unless these were extremely low, till we reached senior classes. Compare that to the children of today, who, from Class I itself, are under pressure to score 90 per cent and above. And they don't have to manage only academic excellence— there are sports, drama, recitation and many other extra-curricular activities, for which their performance is closely monitored.

Of course, this also means that parents are expected to ensure that their child is excelling at everything in the name of 'all-round development'. Parents of today are expected to be more involved—and sometimes this takes the shape of 'helicopter parenting', where even a small aberration in the child's performance causes stress to the child and makes the parents panic.

The exposure to information, sexuality and junk food has led to adolescence setting in much earlier than before. While they are still trying to figure out the nuances of simple mathematics, they now also need to additionally deal with peer pressure as well as the physical and mental changes set off by early puberty.

It's critical to understand two aspects of this age. One, this phase is not easy. There is a lot happening simultaneously:

- Physical growth
- Mental and emotional growth
- Increased academic pressure
- Influence of peers and the need to be a part of the group
- Urge to question everything about society, morals, values, etc.
- Urge to experiment and take risks

The need to be understood, the need for support, the need for a person who would believe in us, someone who would trust us, give us the space to make mistakes and guide us—can we be the person who fulfils these needs for our child? It may seem a daunting task, but if we can build that connection, wouldn't it be wonderful?

Two, it's a phase of transformation—from being a child to being an adult—and that transformation takes six–seven years. Like all transformations, it is difficult, but critical. Everyone has to go through this turmoil and this emotional roller-coaster to grow and develop. What they need is support, not help. The grind of these years is what makes us an adult.

We as parents need to understand that:

- Our children going through this phase is normal. The emotional roller-coaster and their accentuated behaviours are part of the process. It's a critical and integral part of growing up. Everyone has to go through, experience, and grow through this process.
- We need to get into their world: their difficulties, their pain, their exuberance, without judging—not sympathizing, but empathizing.

In this conversation, what Vikas saw for himself was that he was trying to understand his daughter from his perspective, and extrapolating what happened to him when he was her age. He then realized that he first needed to understand what his daughter was going through without judging or evaluating her. In his enthusiasm to be the best father, he had been trying to impose his understanding and his experience of adolescence on his daughter to compensate for the support structure he missed in his teenage years. He also saw that his wife, too, was trying to do the same. He suddenly understood his daughter's space—she was on her own roller-coaster (which, he now saw, was far bigger in terms of the curves and turns); as a father he was on his own trying to figure out her life from his point of view, and his wife had her own perspective. He took to sharing this insight with Tanvi, and then rather than talking to her and asking her about herself, he would talk to her about himself—sharing his life, his journey, his emotional and mental travails, simply creating a space of sharing.

It was the first time Vikas saw the reality of the kind of exposure his daughter and children her age have, and he realized that things are much more difficult now than in past years. The children today have so many resources available—the best of facilities at schools, a larger variety of foods, phones and other gadgets, the internet, Netflix and other streaming platforms, cars and comforts—but greater exposure has also resulted in greater stress levels.

Vikas called a day later and excitedly shared how, when he sat down with his daughter and talked about how difficult it must be for her at her age and times, she started to cry, gave him a hug and said, 'Now you really know what I have to deal with and what I am going through!'

This was just the start Vikas had been looking for. His daughter then opened up to him about the pressures of being a 14 year old. She started to ask him how he had managed the ups and downs, the mood swings and the pressures of being this age. She shared that she believed in their family's value system and really respected her mother for selflessly and relentlessly standing by everyone, for keeping the family's happiness paramount and for instilling values and traditions in them.

Vikas's daughter had been reading about the impact of alcohol and drugs on the body, mind, family and social circles, but in the current state of availability and exposure, it was almost impossible for a teenager to not get into these. She shared how parties were happening at bars, lounges and hotels. Even in parties happening at a friend's house, alcohol and drugs were readily available. There was a lot of peer pressure to try them—to the extent that her friends threatened to ostracize her from the group if she didn't participate. There had been times when she was bullied for days at school for not smoking with them, to the extent that she couldn't get herself to go to school. Vikas remembered how he and his wife had to push Tanvi to go to school on those days. He remembered how he had to literally pick her up and drag her to the car once. That had been a tough interaction—both Vikas and his wife were shouting at her, and Tanvi was not saying anything but wanted to be left alone. It ended up in a slug match and after dropping Tanvi off at the school, the parents had a fight blaming each other for the state Tanvi was in.

Vikas had then failed to understand why Tanvi was behaving that way, but today they had managed to create that space where she could confide in him. This door which Vikas opened for his daughter needs to be opened by all of us for our children. The things that come in the way are our assumptions, our belief systems and our values. We need to understand that these things were created by us, during our times, 30 years ago, and through our own experiences. The current environment of our children is very different. It's almost like we are not on the same planet. The kind of exposure and experiences our children are going through cannot be envisaged or understood by us. What we need is do is acknowledge these differences and learn to listen to our children, with the understanding that they are simply different, not wrong.

ACTION HACK

- Have at least 30 minutes of 'sharing time' twice a week or more, where you share with your children stories of:
  - Your childhood
  - Your pre-teens
  - Your adolescence
  - Your daily life

BONUS

Include your own parents (your child's grandparents) in these sharing sessions, where they too share stories about their childhood, adolescence and early adulthood—and your childhood!

9

YOUR BIGGEST POWER: YOU ARE AN EXAMPLE

Gaurav had been smoking since the time he was in Class XII. What had initially started off as an attempt to impress his friends at school had later become a habit. In fact, in time he had become addicted to smoking, to the point that he had been smoking two packs of cigarettes every day for almost three years. Gaurav's wife Karishma had tried all means to get him to quit smoking. Even the fact that Gaurav had lost his mom to lung cancer did not deter him. He had his arguments—one such being that since his mother never smoked, the cancer had not been caused by smoking.

In our experience, parents are always worried about the impact of society—peers, teachers, friends and the society at large—on their children. And rightly so! If we look at the child's environment, we will realize that the two parents comprise a miniscule percentage of it. With the advent of media—television, live streaming, the internet and social media—and people's propensity to access and use them, the complexities of their environment have increased exponentially. Advertisers and game developers are not only experts in the fields of designing and enticing children and the youth, they are also equipping themselves with child-development learnings to make their product more potent.

The fact that a large number of people and elements in the environment have the power to influence our children's lives makes us feel helpless, as we do not have control over all these elements. The good news is that your power and influence as a parent are not measured by a comparison in numbers—they are far greater and far more potent than all the other elements put together. Most of you may be smirking at this sentence right now, but let us go through a quick exercise to really get a sense of your power as a parent.

Close your eyes and bring to your mind a person in your life whom you admire—someone who has impacted your life, someone from whom you have learnt/picked up skills and attributes. This 'someone' could be your mentor, your boss, a parent, a grandparent, someone from the extended family or even someone you admire but have never met. Notice that this list includes parents, grandparents and other significant adults from the family, alongside other possibilities. Now think of the traits, attributes and skills you have acquired from them. Honesty, love, being selflessly committed to the family and caring for them, being organized, being upright, not giving up, being calm and at peace—the list of attributes that we can pick from the people who feature on this list can go on.

My next question to you is: did you pick up admirable traits from these people just because they talked about them, or because they set an example by living these traits?[*] For example, my father *is* organized, as his immaculate filing system, timely payment of bills and prompt responses to any queries shared with him would reflect—add to this that he

---

[*]https://www.youtube.com/watch?v=qya0abzYrws

would have a paper trail for everything too!

Now, let me give you some bad news.

As a parent, you do not have a choice when it comes to being an example. You *are* a living example to your children— and there is no way out of that role. They won't do what you tell them to do; they will do what *you do*. Now, that may seem like a lot of pressure, for we need to watch out for whatever we say and do, as they will copy us. That is only one of the two ways to look at the situation—the other being that your being an example puts you in a position of power, where you can influence your child to do what you deem appropriate. If you see them doing something that you don't approve of, step back and check if any of the significant adults in your child's life is doing the same thing.

Let me share an example. Many parents have argued with me regarding screen time. They say that while they spend just about an hour after coming home either checking official emails and messages or watching news or infotainment channels, their children take as much as five–six hours of screen time—from playing online games with their friends to watching cartoons and other shows. So, according to these parents, if they *are* an example for their children, why are their children not limiting their screen time to, say, an hour, as they do?

We need to understand the logic. For children, it is not the question of one hour or five. How they see it is that their parents spend their 'free' time on the screen and so do they—the only difference being that while parents have only an hour of free time, they have five–six. So, the equation is not one hour equals five hours, but that 'free' time equals screen time. Moreover, parents spend their screen time doing what they like (or what they need to, in the case of emails), and they do the same. Cartoons and online games have the same charm for children that news and infotainment have for adults.

So, before you dismiss this power you have, keep aside everything and sit back for 10 minutes to reflect on the following:

- Make a list of positive actions and behaviour patterns that your child has been copying from you. Pat yourself for doing these, as your child has picked up this stuff without you having to specifically train them, and ensure you keep doing these things.

- Similarly, make a list of negative actions and behaviour patterns that your child has been imbibing from you. It could be the way you talk to your domestic helps, your parents, your siblings or your spouse, your screen time, time spent (or lack thereof) on learning things or towards an exercise routine to keep fit and so on. Make a conscious effort towards breaking these habits and behaviour patterns.

- Make a list of behaviours you would want your child to imbibe or things you would want them to follow, but which you are not doing yourself. These could be things you always wanted to do or change in yourself. You may not have had big enough reasons to do them, or something might have been stopping you. But now you have the reason—your child. Things that we wouldn't do for ourselves, we do for them. Start learning these new behaviours and lead by example; your child may follow in time.

Remember that if you and your spouse show different behaviour patterns, your child is likely to take after the one they find more convenient!

When we discussed the role of parents as role models for their children at a programme run for parents by Parwarish, the discussion had a profound impact on Gaurav. He realized that he has the biggest impact on his son, and he cannot be a role model who inspires his son to smoke. This thought set off a chain of events in the lives of Gaurav and Karishma. Gaurav spent the next three to four days researching the impact of smoking and was shocked by the results of his research. In 2016 alone, tobacco use caused over 7.1 million deaths worldwide (5.1 million in men, 2 million in women). Most of these deaths (6.3 million) were attributable to direct cigarette smoking, followed by second-hand smoke (8,84,000 deaths).

This made Gaurav decide that he would quit smoking and become an example for his son Neil. It has been more than 18 months, and Gaurav has not only quit smoking, he also encourages his friends to do the same. In fact, he has even created a short film on his journey from being addicted to smoking to becoming a non-smoker. The movie, available on YouTube,* has received positive responses, with many people writing to Gaurav to give him credit for their decision to quit smoking.

That's the power you have—you can not only transform your life and that of those in your immediate social circle—you also have the ability to impact millions.

---

*https://www.youtube.com/watch?v=CmAuRXGqEgw&t=24s

ACTION HACK

We often see and feel that our children are not doing something we want them to do, or doing something that we don't want them to do. Sit back and reflect on which action of yours is being replicated. Don't look at it from the point of view of blame, but with the intention of identifying and attaining the power within yourself to make the much-needed shift.

10

KNOWING THE CHILD,
KNOWING OURSELVES

The most profound change in Monica and my life came when we became parents. From being a couple who didn't feel the urge to be parents to one that finds the parenting journey a joyous and fulfilling experience—our ideas, just as our life, underwent a shift.

Let's do a quick exercise that will give you a sense of who this child is—the child for whom you picked up this book. Think of a real two-and-a-half to three-year-old child. Do not do this exercise with an imaginary child or by reimagining yourself as one. Answer the next few questions specifically for that child:

- Are they mostly happy? (Whether it's sunny or raining, whether it's morning or night, whether they are in a train or in the park, they are mostly happy.)
- Are there times when they come across as not being happy? (There are times when they are not happy. At these times they are expressing themselves—whether they are angry, adamant or sad, they express themselves without any fear or inhibitions. They are completely self-expressed.)

- How do you rate their self-confidence? (I rate them 20 out of 10—yes, at 200 per cent! This is because they want to try even those things they are aware they don't know. For example, they are the ones who always want to drive—they will sit on the driver's seat and ask us to sit at the back, knowing very well that they cannot drive. If we ask them if they can cook food, their response is likely to be a resounding yes!)
- How many questions do they ask? (Children of this age group ask unlimited questions. They have a question for everything they see, hear, touch or taste. 'How', 'why', 'what', 'when' and 'where' are the most often used words. They are inquisitive. It gets exasperating listening to and trying to answer their questions. Usually the questions are unanswerable!)
- How do you rate their exploration ability? (If you observe them closely, you would find that these kids are always exploring—touching, tasting, even breaking stuff to see how they work. They are explorers, going around and investigating everything they can lay their eyes and hands on.)
- Do they ever give up? (Once they set their minds and hearts on something, these children don't seem to give up. Our strategies to distract them also fail; as soon as the distraction is over, they invariably go back to what they were pursuing.)
- Do they want to do everything themselves? (These children, even though they are unable to do a lot of things, want to do everything themselves. They strive to be self-reliant—they want to feed themselves, even if they are spilling most of the food on their clothes

or on the floor; they want to take baths on their own and dress up by themselves, without help from adults.)

- At what level would you rate their self-esteem? (Children of this age group refer to themselves by their own name,—that is, they talk of themselves in the third person. Instead of saying 'I am hungry', they would say, 'Sushant is hungry'. The child development experts of yesteryears interpreted this behaviour as ego-centric behaviour. The Parwarish model interprets this as reflecting high self-esteem. These children perceive themselves as being the centre of the universe, and view themselves as capable of everything.)
- Are they loving and caring? (Children at this age are bundles of love and affection. Being humane comes naturally to them. Concern for their parents, pets, etc. is inborn.)

This may sound incredible, but they are all of the above.

During the first couple of years of Aman's life, our focus was entirely on his well-being. As he grew up, we keenly observed him. A few observations really opened our eyes to the miraculous creation called 'human being'.

We used to travel a lot when Aman was young. I was personally struck by his sheer exuberance and excitement in any situation. Be it in a restaurant, on a railway platform waiting for a much-delayed train or travelling by road in a car, he would be happy, running around, playing. In comparison, we would be looking at the watch every few minutes, complaining about the delays, the time, the weather and just about everything. What struck me the most is that neither his nor our reactions to the situation changed the situation itself. But our respective experiences of the situation were poles apart. We as adults were blaming what was happening outside of us and having a stressful time; he, on the other hand, was doing what was in his control and enjoying the time. Neither his reaction nor ours could influence the situation, but they altered our experience of life in those moments. He was proof of the fact that our happiness, and the power to enjoy the present, lie within us.

With that, I became an avid—or should I say obsessed— observer of parents and children in every situation. I would see how children at traffic signals, the homeless ones who lived under flyovers and those who accompanied their manual labourer parents at construction sites would be enjoying themselves with whatever they could lay their hands on—a piece of cloth, a damaged tyre, a piece of paper crushed to form a ball; they may have been unbathed and wearing torn clothes, and yet they were truly happy.

This ability to find happiness within is innate in every child, and fades as we become adults. My observations made me wonder if I could relearn and rekindle this innate quality that I had lost in the course of gaining adulthood. In these seemingly little ways, our journey as parents, or rather our journey as disciples, started after Aman was born—and it began transforming our experience of life.

While Aman had that innate quality of finding happiness in the most wearisome of situations, there were also times when he would throw tantrums, wail and howl. Taking his favourite toy away from him temporarily could also trigger such a tantrum. There were times we would feel embarrassed by his shows of emotion. For instance, once I had a family outing to the movies with my colleagues from my then workplace. My boss, my peers, as well as my juniors had all come with their respective families. In the middle of the movie, when a serious scene was playing on screen, Aman started to laugh out loud—loud enough to be heard across the movie hall. At first I reacted like an embarrassed father would, with an expression of apology on my face, but it soon turned into a smile of realization—I realized my son's unhindered ability to express himself, irrespective of the place or the situation, unaffected by those around him and what they may think of him. What a beautiful sense of freedom that must have been!

Our daughter Vaanya too had that innate sense of self-confidence as a young child. When she was three years old, she would be the first one to run to the kitchen to get water for her grandfather. When stopped, she would turn around and say that she would open the refrigerator to take out the water bottle and climb on the shelf to grab a glass. She would act out how she would then pour the water and take it to her grandfather. She made it all sound so simple, but as adults we were scared that she wouldn't be able to hold a glass bottle full of water and pour it into a glass. Regardless, she definitely had the confidence that she could! There would be times when we would have to hold her back from igniting the gas burner to cook. In her opinion, she could do whatever she saw her mother or grandmother do. She would even mimic them and tell us that she could cook, because she knew how to! Vaanya's confidence at that age was envious—it was miraculously greater than my confidence in delivering a presentation at work for which I had prepared and rehearsed well.

One of the things that we would sometimes find wearisome was the number of questions these children had. Even after you responded to one of their questions, they would always come back with a counter-question! A typical conversation would go like:

Aman: Who is this person in the photograph?

Me: That's my grandfather.

Aman: Where is he? I haven't seen him ever.

Me: He's not alive anymore.

Aman: What do you mean by not alive?
(At this point, I would wonder how to explain to a three-year-old what it means to not be alive. As a diligent father, I was determined to answer this question in the most authentic manner. But alas, it was a tough one!)

Me: He was old. And when we get old, our body deteriorates and one day we die.

Aman: At what age do people die? What happens when one dies?

Me: There is no specific age.

By that time I was at my wits end and his enthusiasm was increasing. I was trying hard not to get irritated. And the fact was that he was not trying to irritate me; these were genuine questions. I realized that this would be a never-ending conversation. This wasn't the only time. Every time he saw something, a barrage of questions would follow:

- What is this animal?
- Why is it barking? It is different from the animal you called 'dog' the last time.
- Who is this person?

- Why is he smiling?
- Where are we going?
- Why are we going there?
- Which colour is this?

The insatiable quest for knowledge at that age is unbelievable. Parents get irritated and exasperated with the never-ending questions. We often wonder where they get these questions from. The fact is that they are born inquisitive. Anything that they see, hear, smell, touch or even dream of, triggers a question in their mind. They want to know more about it, and one question leads to another. This is the quest of humankind, which has led to all the development in the world.

There is a story about Albert Einstein—that he was a slow learner during his childhood. When asked about how he could become such a discoverer in his lifetime, he said that his inquisitiveness as a child continued into his adulthood when he could start to find answers to his own questions!

This inquisitiveness and urge to explore are innate in us. We are born with them, but we often forget to acknowledge and nurture these qualities as we move into adulthood.

When Aman was around six months old, one afternoon, I was playing with him. He had just started to crawl on his stomach. I was playing this little game with him, where I would place his rattler a foot away from him, and he would take about three to five minutes to crawl through that 10–12 inch distance and somehow reach the rattler, which he would celebrate with a toothless smile of pride. I would then take the rattler and place it another feet away from him. This continued for a long time. He seemed to enjoy the game, and I could see that he was learning to crawl, which gave me a sense of pride too. What opened up for me that day altered my life forever. Imagine someone doing this to us as adults, taking away what we have achieved after a lot of hard work and urging us to do the hard work again to get it. We would have smashed the person and perhaps walked away from the situation. And here was a six-month-old kid who just wouldn't give up. In the process, he was building his muscles, his capacity, and teaching me the lesson of 'never giving up'. That day, he made me realize that if our children are unable to access and experience their 'nolimitness', they would never realize what a privilege it is to be born human. And that became our dream—for not just our own children, Aman and Vaanya, but for every parent and child we could reach out to. That was the birth of the Parwarish Institute of Parenting.

Some of you may say that the 'nolimitness' is not true for all children—that there are exceptions. My request would be to go a bit deeper into the lives of these exceptions and see how these elements got suppressed or damaged at such an early age.

In our experience over the last 10 years with children and parents in various communities cutting across cultures, socio-economic strata and even countries, this has been a common observation. Whether it's been the tribal Bheel community, or the children of ragpickers, beggars and daily wagers, or those of Japanese, Chinese or American parents, that's just how children are—born with no limits.

Imagine a child with such qualities. Now imagine if these qualities can be saved from the ravages of adulthood and life. What we would get would be happy, healthy, responsible and unstoppable human beings! All we need to do as parents is ensure that the qualities the children were all born with are not suppressed or damaged. At the same time, we need to train ourselves to nurture these qualities in our children—providing them with stimulating and nurturing environments that help them in actualizing their unlimited potential, growing up to be happy, healthy, responsible and unstoppable adults.

Is this conversation making you feel that you have suppressed or damaged these qualities inadvertently? Do you sense a feeling of guilt creeping in? Or are you in denial? You may wonder if all this would even hold for children who are differently abled—those born with congenital defects, Autism, Down's Syndrome, physical disabilities, learning disabilities and so on.

This is a myth-breaking conversation and the feelings and thoughts of disbelief or disagreement at this point are valid. The idea is to open ourselves up to the immense possibilities that have remained ignored so far.

ACTION HACK

Observe your children and their behaviour closely for the next few days. Observe them through the new lens of 'nolimitness'. Look for the following behavioural traits in them:

1. Being happy.
2. Being self-expressed. Even if they are expressing themselves unabashedly with one person in their life, they may appear to be 'introverted' or 'shy'. See where all and with whom they are expressing themselves openly.
3. Being confident. This confidence could be in any area.
4. Being self-reliant/responsible. This could be them wanting to do some activities on their own or taking care of their sibling or their favourite toy, game, book, etc.
5. Being inquisitive. Look at all the areas they are inquisitive about—their quest for information and knowledge in those areas.

6. Being explorers. See how they go out of their way to explore certain things in life. These could even be areas that attract them, or them wanting to break and open up things to see what's inside.

7. Never giving up. This may show up as their tenacity in general in games, activities, etc., but can also show up as their 'stubbornness'. Being stubborn is at the root of not giving up. They have their thoughts and their requirements, and they would do anything to fulfil them.

The areas in which you are able to observe these traits and qualities may not be appropriate from our point of view. I am not justifying these actions nor do I want you to justify these.

Also, make a note even if you see these qualities in 1 per cent of these areas. The idea is to really become aware of the qualities in them, with the intention of nurturing them. If we are able to create an environment where we can nurture these qualities in productive areas, think of the immense potential life would have for them and for you.

11

YES, YOU CAN!

Instilling Self-belief—the Source of Their Performance

Our opinions of our children shape the way they think about themselves. In this chapter, we will find out how a child's self-esteem determines the course of their life and how we can nurture it—or rather how we can undo the damage that we (as parents) and the external environment cause to a child's self-esteem.

As our kids—and we—grow, they start acquiring a personality. These personality traits are products of:

- Circumstances
- Upbringing
- Reactions of people around us—parents, grandparents, other significant adults, siblings, etc.
- How we respond to situations
- Perceptions of the people around us
- Our perceptions of ourselves

These interactions start to create elements of personality, which become our strengths or weaknesses—things we feel we are capable of and things that become our limitations. These elements come in the way of experiencing the innate unlimited potential of being human. From a child with 'unlimited potential', we end up becoming a certain personality type with limited capabilities. It is critical for us to realize that as parents we have the power to undo this damage. The exercise that follows will help us understand this at a fundamental level. Here, we will examine our key personality traits. Use the format given below to list down the words different people use to describe you. Be brutally honest.

How do people describe me?

Self	Parents	Spouse	In-laws	Friends	People who don't like me

Once you have filled up the chart, you will realize:

- There are certain traits that are common between the various columns.
- There are certain adjectives that people tend to associate with you, which you would agree with.
- There are certain traits that people associate with you, but you don't agree with.
- There are certain contradictory traits that different people associate with you. For instance, someone may find you to be open and forthcoming, while another may find you closed and reserved—this differs because

we may respond differently to different people, based on the situation and our personal equations with them.

While we may or may not agree with some of the words that people use to describe us, it doesn't matter. These reflect people's perceptions of us—how they individually see us and relate to us.

Now, take any one of the traits and answer the following questions:

- Do you display this trait all the time? For instance, are you identified as an introvert by everyone around you—your family, friends and colleagues—or do you display this trait only with certain individuals or groups?
- If it is not a trait you consistently display round the clock, how often and how long would you say you display this trait, in terms of percentage?
- How many times and in what situations have you behaved differently—maybe diametrically opposite—to this trait?

These questions are bound to induce some doubts about the solidity of these traits. We certainly project these traits. However, I am sure you can cite examples of not displaying these traits in certain situations and with certain people. For example, people in my extended family often tell me that I am a very quiet person, but those in my professional sphere tend to say that I talk a lot and have an opinion about everything. So, what's the sanctity of these traits? Are these actually fixed traits or adaptable behaviour (behaviours that change, based on the situation and the people)?

The idea behind this conversation is to understand that we, and the people around us, attach certain personality traits to ourselves which are not fixed, but fall on a spectrum of behaviours.

We have been living with these traits. A few of them restrict us, limit our capacity, make us stop mid-course. Others may define our strengths at a certain level, but restrict us by taking away the flexibility of having alternative responses to a situation. These traits hold us back from exploring and experiencing the entire gamut of traits, strengths, weaknesses, opportunities and so on.

Let's recall an exercise we did previously—wherein we observed the qualities of a two-and-a-half to three-year-old and a six-month-old child. Children at that age are full of unlimited potential, with no specific traits limiting them (unless we have given them a few even at that age!).

We are born that way—without the labels that limit us. That's the real us. Before we get into seeing how these labels became an integral part of us, let's do an exercise to experience the power of removing these labels. I would urge you to do this exercise without judgment—just experience it.

Tear off each trait from the list you wrote for yourself, one by one, and while doing so, imagine that they are being pulled off of you, thereby freeing you from the constraints that they have imposed all these years. This will take you back to the experience of the child you once were, with all the possibilities of life.

Say to yourself: 'I am No-limit (your name). These are labels and I am distinct from all labels.'

Let's look at how these behaviours and actions taken during the early years became our personality and eventually define who we are.

The actions—or inactions—of our early years led to our

parents and other people around us describing us in certain ways. The traits assigned to us by others are thus based on our behaviour. Let me share my story.

During the early years—it must have started when I was three years old—instead of walking, I would always run and jump around. This led to my parents and grandparents calling me fidgety and impatient. I would pick up stuff and drop it, which led to them calling me clumsy—and of course they would try to keep things out of my reach. Each of these adjectives was being given to me by the most significant people in my life. As I grew up, my being upfront was tagged as being 'short-tempered'. By the time I was 20, I was complete with my set of traits—boxed in as a fidgety, impatient, headstrong, clumsy, short-tempered, compassionate, happy-go-lucky guy, to mention a few strong traits that people associated with me. These traits helped me succeed in many situations, but they also limited me in others.

The aforementioned exercise of tearing off traits from the list has not only helped me in my individual capacity, I have seen it bring back power to thousands of parents and children we have worked with—the power to be whatever they wanted to be, and to let go of all constraints put in by the labels given to us.

A question for you: are these words describing you or your behaviour? The question sounds simple but creates a very critical distinction. Are we our behaviour? That's what happens. When we keep dropping stuff, *we*—and not our *behaviour*—are labelled as clumsy; when we lose our cool and get angry (even if it is once a week), they say, 'He/She is short-tempered' rather than, 'He/She lost his/her temper.'

Hearing this from the significant adults in our life—our

parents, grandparents, teachers—makes it even more powerful. The people who introduced us to ourselves—who told us our date and time of birth, our name and gender—also told us who 'we' are as per our behaviour. They slowly cut through the whole gamut of behaviours, narrowing down to a few into which we are boxed.

From today onwards, practise labelling the behaviour as opposed to labelling yourself.

Having experienced the power of de-labelling yourself, let's move to the power we have as parents over the nolimitness of our children.

Let's go ahead and remove every label we have for them and they have for themselves, unpeeling and bringing forth the unlimited potential they were born with. This process won't be easy on two counts:

- We are wired to make judgments and by default, we label the person instead of the behaviour. So, we would have to be conscious and practise it for a long time before we get the hang of it.
- Keep removing the labels that we acquire/collect periodically. I recommend doing this exercise once a month to ensure that you and the child are able to build a space for yourselves.

While doing this exercise with herself at a workshop conducted by Parwarish, Surabhi started crying. When we asked her the reason, she shared with us that for the last two years the teachers in her son's school had been complaining that Akash was 'slow'. In all the parent–teachers meetings they had been telling the parents that Akash was not able to finish off his classwork, he was not able to write down his homework completely and he had never been able to complete his tests in time.

For the last two years, they had been cajoling Akash to write fast. They had been telling him that he was slow and prodding him to practise every day to improve his speed. Despite the efforts made by them and the teachers, who now made him sit next to them to help him write, there had been no improvement. The situation had actually gone from bad to worse. Not only had his performance declined, he was now reluctant to write. The teachers then started insisting on getting him assessed for a probable learning disability. Rahul and Surabhi had taken an appointment with a centre for Akash's assessment, which was due the next week.

The same day, Surabhi and Rahul did this exercise with Akash. They told him that he was not slow, that it was just a label put on him by them and the teachers. They told him he was capable of doing anything. They didn't stop at this. The next day, they met the teacher and requested her to change her communication with Akash. They requested that whenever Akash was not writing well, she should tell him, 'you are no-limit and you can do it'.

This little shift worked like magic. Two days later, Akash returned home excited—he had finished his classwork well in time and the teacher appreciated him for doing something that he hadn't ever done before. That was the day Akash tore off the label of being slow. His speed, handwriting and performance has kept improving from that day onwards. All that Rahul and Surabhi have continued to do is to keep telling him that he is a no-limit child, and he is capable of everything!

Parents who have gone through the process in our programmes have benefitted from it. I would want you, too, to adopt the approach and see how it works wonders for you.

ACTION HACK

Do this exercise with each other as a family. It may appear stupid and frivolous at the start, but the idea is to realize the absurdity of labels. Someone tells us who we are and then we start responding to that label.

- Identify and articulate your and your children's labels.
- Put them on your body and their's, using post-its.
- Then remove them.
- Call yourself and your children 'no-limit'.
- Take an action in an area you earlier thought you couldn't.
- Experience the magic!

12

NEGOTIATING WITH OUR CHILDREN

It is either their way or our way. Many parents these days feel that when they were young, they had to give in (to their parents) and now they still have to give in (to their children)!

As a parent, there is a very high chance that you have said these words a million times:

'Eat your vegetables'

'Put the video game away and complete your homework'

'Shut the computer and go and play outside'

You would have also heard the following responses a million times:

'My stomach hurts'

'I'll do it tomorrow'

'Just 10 more minutes'

Life with children is an ongoing negotiation—be it about sleeping on time, studying or screen time. The word 'negotiation' sounds like a bad word. Should you be negotiating with your children at all? But whether you like it or not, you do negotiate with them.

Negotiating with children is a challenging process and if not done right, it leads to unhappiness and frustration. As parents, you may feel you gave in too early, while your children may feel they had no say in the matter. Whatever the outcome, someone is always unhappy. So, how can you negotiate more successfully with your children?

Let's look at some of the negotiation skills we use at work to resolve issues, and see how we can translate these into negotiating with our children at home. At work, we usually proceed with a plan that involves initiating a discussion, identifying the problem at hand, discussing possible solutions and listing them down, analysing all the solutions to narrow down on one, implementing the solution, and reviewing it at a later date to assess its effectiveness and tweaking it, if required.

These things normally come naturally to us when we are at work. Now let's apply this, step-by-step, to our situation at home.

Step 1—Initiate a discussion: Get together in a room with your child and initiate a discussion on the issue at hand. You could start with something like, 'So, here's a situation. Let's figure out how we should resolve it.' By not accusing the child of having a problem, you are avoiding a situation where the child might get defensive right at the start. The problem/issue is not with the child—it's an issue you are dealing with together. This discussion needs to be initiated during 'peace time'—that is, not while you are busy dealing with the particular situation. Find an appropriate time when you and your child are not in a space of heightened emotions.

Step 2—Identify the problem clearly: It's important to state the problem clearly. For example, if the problem is that the child is watching TV for three hours every day, then first look at what the problem really is. Watching TV in itself cannot be a problem. The problem would be its impact on the child, in the following ways:

- The damage on eyesight
- The quality of the programmes
- The language/visuals of the programmes
- The lack of time for other activities and so on

So identifying what the real problem is and putting it on the table is the key to this process. More often than not, we end up discussing the symptoms or the behaviour, and not the real problem.

At the same time, remember not to club issues together. For example, you may say, 'You are playing too many video games and that's why you are not getting good grades.' If that's actually the case, then state it, but if playing video games is either not clearly the reason for low grades or not the only reason for low grades, then don't link the two. Be specific to the problem at hand.

Step 3—Write down everyone's ideas: Make a list of all the ideas proposed during the discussion. Remember not to reject or criticize any idea, however bizarre it may sound. While sharing ideas, listen to your child's point of view—it's a valid point of view.

Step 4—Discuss all the ideas and narrow down to a solution: Once all the ideas are on the table, you can start to narrow down to a solution. With consensus, delete, add or club ideas together to identify a few possible solutions. It may not always be possible to narrow down to one solution, but through discussion, everyone can be persuaded to try one out to start with.

Step 5—Assign responsibilities: Once the solution is decided, it is important to run through how it will be implemented, so that everyone knows what they are supposed to do and by when.

Step 6—Build deterrents: Deterrents are 'consequences' that are agreed on beforehand. These ensure that we do what we agreed to, else we bear the consequences of not keeping our promises. Without a feasible and strong enough deterrent, we may go back to our old ways.

Step 7—Propose a review of the solution: Propose a review date for the solution to see how well it is working. This gives you an option to revisit the solution and make changes, if it is not working, to make it more effective.

This approach targets the problem and not the persons involved—whether parents or children. This prevents any resentment from brewing between the two, and has the following advantages:

- It derives solutions through consensus, making the children feel involved in the decision-making process. This makes it more likely to succeed.
- The ideation and open discussion help build trust between parents and children.
- It trains children in resolving issues amicably in life.

So, next time you negotiate with your children, remember that negotiation is not about winning or losing. It is about exploring options objectively and creating a win-win situation for all.

13

YOU ARE YOU: NO COMPARISONS

The 10-letter word 'comparison' can best be described using a four-word phrase—'destroyer of human potential'.

Our scriptures talk about the potential of humans being unlimited—'*Sarv gun sampan* (bearing all qualities)' is how everyone is born. Then, at some point, we start thinking of ourselves as being less than that—and we start running in this never-ending race of proving ourselves better than others.

The game starts with small comparisons between siblings made by parents—it could be about a child's slow speed vis-à-vis their sibling when it comes to eating or getting ready, or lack of focus while following instructions or studying. There is no measurement for human potential. However, since we, as humans, are obsessed with measurements, we have built certain markers to measure the potential of individuals. They may not be direct and accurate measures of such potential, but they provide us with something to hold on to in the uncertain world we live in. We thus tend to measure the potential not only of children, but also of adults.

A few measures by which we map the potential of a child are:

- How much the person is scoring in the subjects we decided to teach them

- How much time they take to finish their meals
- How much time they take to get ready
- How much time they take to finish their homework or assignments
- How they talk to elders
- Whether they comply with the norms set by the society

This kind of mapping is the elders' attempt to gauge a child's potential, their ability to 'do well' in the future and be happy. Since there is no thermometer to measure the exact state of these abilities, where the child stands in comparison to other children their age or where the adults were at that age becomes the only way to measure their potential.

Similarly, we also tend to measure the potential of adults. Some key measures of their potential are:

- What position/designation they hold in their career
- How much they earn
- The size and make of their house, car, TV, mobile phone and so on
- The brand of clothes they wear
- Where and how often they eat out, travel and so on
- How good they look

All of these supposedly measure happiness. The issue is that there is no absolute measure of any of the above—so the way out is a comparative measure!

We often see that a person is happy with their resources (salary, position, car, house, etc.) as long as they are better than most—if not all—in their social circle. What this, in effect, implies is that a person's happiness is a factor only of the happiness of others around them. Now reflect on this: these measures are destroying self-esteem, self-confidence, creativity and the ability to venture out and take risks, not only in children but also in adults. This lays emphasis on conformity or the need to fit in, which comes from the continuous need to prove oneself better than the other and, in the process, kills the humane qualities of compassion and love, while bringing a lot of stress to our lives.

As parents, we have a choice—a choice whether to believe in our child, in their individuality, their unlimited potential (immeasurable because it is limitless) or push through never-ending comparisons, which can kill their spirit as they try to fit in as per the norms.

Let us break this vicious cycle and create a no-limit world of happiness and expression for every child.

Sibling Rivalry

Sibling rivalry can simply be defined as the feeling of competition between two or more siblings. This can occur due to many factors, like parental behaviour towards each child, order of birth, age gap between the siblings and so on.

Sibling rivalry starts with the arrival of the second child. When the second child is born, they need attention and care. Considering the vulnerability of the newborn, both the parents give more attention to this child, showering them with love and affection, fulfilling their basic needs like feeding, cuddling and kissing them and so on. The relatives too show excitement and express love and affection for the new arrival. In all this, we sometimes forget to observe how it is affecting the older child. Often the older child thinks the parents don't love them anymore—or not as much as the younger sibling. There is a natural shift of attention towards the baby, but the older child is unable to understand the logical reasoning behind it. This sometimes leads to the older child developing some degree of hatred towards the younger sibling, as they hold the younger sibling responsible for their own dethroning from being the centre of the parents' lives. It is not uncommon to hear of older siblings trying to hit the baby or pushing them off the bed. My mother told me I'd hit my younger sister when my mom wasn't around, who would run to our mother, wailing. All this is very common, and yet we tend to overlook this important psychological impact of the birth of another child on the older one.

This sibling rivalry is further accentuated when parents start comparing the children on various fronts. As parents, we are always looking at the scope of improvement in our kids. Many times, this takes the form of comparative assessments between two or more children, with the weaker one being prodded to perform like the stronger one. We think telling a child that they must try to emulate a sibling—or any other child for that matter—would be a motivating factor. But is it?

It isn't just parents who unconsciously end up comparing siblings; even relatives and teachers tend to do so. We compare how they stand, walk, talk, at what time they get up, how they study, the marks they get, their eating habits, their looks, their behaviour—it's a never-ending list.

It is not uncommon for these sibling rivalries to get to a point where they affect the quality of the relationship between the siblings as adults.

Here are some rules we need to follow to ensure we are not—consciously or unconsciously—laying the seeds of difficult relationships between our children.

Rule 1: No comparison[*]

Every child is born with unlimited potential and everyone is different. How each child sees, listens, learns, interprets is different.

Rule 2: Prepare

Prepare the child well in advance, before the newborn's arrival. Explain to them how their younger sibling would need more attention in the early days and how, while this may seem to impact the time the parents are able to devote to the elder child, it will not affect their love for them.

Rule 3: Team up

The new child is the collective responsibility of the entire family. Involve the elder child in bringing up their sibling— have them support you in feeding the newborn and getting them ready; encourage the elder child to play with the younger sibling; get them to babysit. Make the older child a partner in raising the younger one.

While we have now learnt the way forward, how do we undo the damage that has already been done? To make things better:

- Share with the elder child the reasons for the attention diversion in the early phase of their sibling's arrival— that it was a natural phenomenon and that they too received just as much attention when they were born.

---

[*]https://www.youtube.com/watch?v=1KljnZZxDJM

- Apologize for the comparisons made.
- Set a new rule of 'No Comparisons'—a rule with no exceptions.

Comparison: A Case Study

I received a call from Pallavi, a parent who had got our reference from her daughter's school. We had conducted a session with the teachers on the difficulties children face in learning. She shared with us how her daughter, Varsha, a student of Class VII, was facing issues at school. She was struggling with French, math and science; in other subjects like English and social studies too, she was barely managing to pass her exams. On discussing the matter further, I came to know that Varsha had been in a different school till the previous year and her performance in academics hadn't been this bad at the previous school.

The parents had taken a decision to change her school because there had been consistent complaints about her behaviour—the parents had been told that there was something wrong with Varsha; the way she would walk, talk, interact and even dance were reported to be awkward. Her classmates in the previous school would tease her and had started to isolate her. Things had reached a point where Varsha no longer wanted to go to the school. Hence the change.

Pallavi also shared that she wouldn't allow Varsha to dance at family gatherings. A couple of years ago, Varsha had prepared for a dance to be performed by her at her uncle's wedding, and everyone around had commented on her awkward style of dancing. Pallavi had felt embarrassed and she didn't allow Varsha to dance again.

Moving to a new school allowed Varsha some space, but in time, the teachers and classmates there too had started to single her out. The situation had come to a point where one of the teachers had a long discussion with the parents to tell them that Varsha would not be able to go beyond Class VII. She recommended to the parents that they start looking for some alternatives beyond education for Varsha. This had completely broken Pallavi.

Apparently, Varsha's problem was her style—but was it? The fact was that her style was different and her body movements were awkward *when compared to others*. We are quick to identify a person or a specific aspect of their personality as not being normal. But what are the criteria of 'normal', and where do these so-called standards come from?

Essentially, what is most common is termed as 'normal' by the society. This relativistic approach is at the base of how the society maps people. In a different situation, the norms would change. For instance, examine the definitions of tall, short, thin, fat, beautiful, ugly, handsome, dark, fair and so on across different countries and cultures. There are no absolute measures for any of these—everything is in contrast. Without an appropriate comparison, these adjectives lose their meanings.

Varsha was being termed as awkward on these very grounds—she was different from the others. The difference was being packaged as odd, not normal. Pallavi and her husband Vaibhav realized this and soon started appreciating Varsha's uniqueness.

This is a paradox of life: we try to do something different to prove to people that we are unique, and yet we want to fit in when it comes to how society perceives us.

To extend this conversation further, let's examine the case of:

- Gifted children
- Slow children

Are these categories not based on certain norms human beings have developed by studying what is most common and formulating acceptable standard? Anyone different from what society perceives as 'normal' is tagged as either 'gifted' or 'slow'—depending on which side of the societal spectrum they fall.

Gifted children are provided better facilities, better coaches, better facilitators and more exposure, which leads to widening the gap between the 'normal' and them. On the other hand, 'slow children' are taken off certain activities and certain subjects, and provided individual attention and support, which reduces exposure and creates dependence. But isn't it true that:

- If someone takes more time to acquire a skill, they need more time and greater exposure?
- If you tell someone that they can do it and provide them opportunities to fail—and then to succeed—they may become less dependent with time?

I am not saying that we shouldn't provide better facilities, better coaches, better facilitators and more exposure to the 'gifted'. What I am saying is that let's not withdraw opportunities and facilities from those we perceive as slow simply because we think they can't cope. We only end up making them feel excluded and increasing their dependence by doing so.

The first thing that Pallavi and Vaibhav did was to apologize to Varsha for comparing her with others and making her feel that her style was inferior or wrong. They then set up a special dance performance by Varsha at the next family gathering. They called the dance style Varsha's style. When they appreciated her in front of everyone, everyone started appreciating the uniqueness of Varsha's style, which restored her self-esteem. The results were encouraging: her posture and walk (she had started displaying a bit of a stoop), her eye contact with people and her participation at school transformed. She felt confident about asking and answering questions and her academic performance saw significant improvement. The teachers were shocked, not merely surprised, to see this transformation. From being the 'I can't' and 'something is wrong with me' girl, Varsha became an 'I can' girl.

During this three-month transformative journey of Varsha, Pallavi and Vaibhav went through their own journey of self-blame—they blamed themselves for the damage they had caused over the last five years. They had to be spoken to about this. They did not intentionally take any actions to hurt Varsha. As parents, we make comparisons not with the purpose of damaging our children, but that of motivating them, in our zeal to get the best out of them and make them better at everything. The only issue is that this process doesn't work. And blaming yourself doesn't resolve anything; the idea is to take responsibility, repair the damage and move on.

To understand this paradox at a deeper level, think of the times when you were compared with someone else. This comparison could have been with:

- Your sibling
- Your cousin
- Your neighbour
- Your friend
- Your classmate
- Your parent
- Anyone else

This comparison could have been when you were:

- A child
- A pre-teen
- A teenager
- A young adult
- An adult

The comparison could have been for:

- Your academic performance
- Sports
- Physical attributes such as height, weight, complexion, hair, etc.
- Your way of dressing or hairstyle
- Your skills
- Your salary
- Things that represent your material wealth, such as house, car and so on

Once you have listed such incidents, try to put a finger on how they made you feel. For this, you may refer to the wheel of emotions created by the psychologist Robert Plutchik.[*]

---

*https://www.youtube.com/watch?v=IMTOdO4iTc4&t=1s

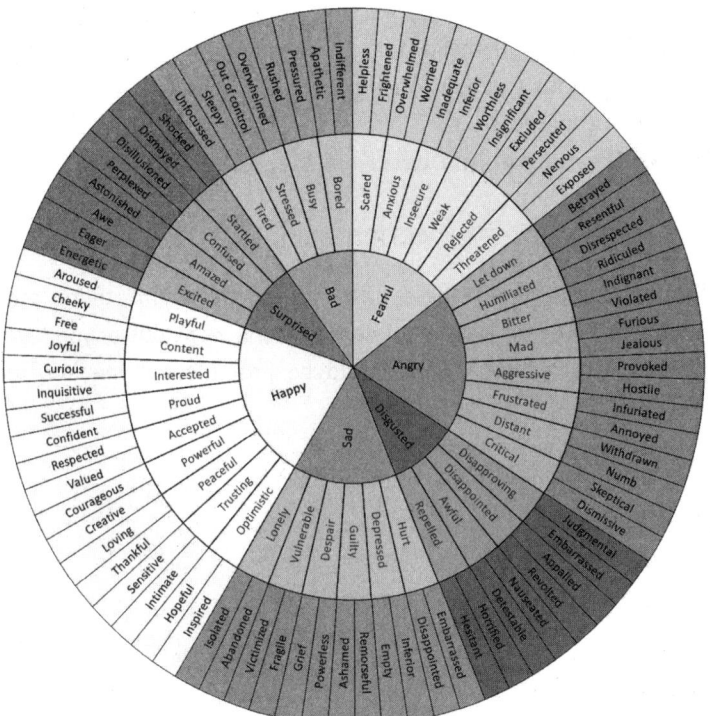

Now also think of the following:

- How did they affect your relationship with the people who made these comparisons?
- How did they affect your relationship with the people you were compared to?

The paradox is that we all use comparisons to motivate, but comparisons leave you with regret, blame, anger, aggression, powerlessness, and feeling unloved or lonely. Even when you are compared favourably,

- It creates a huge pressure to perform and keep the level up all the time.
- It spoils the relationship with the person you are being compared to.
- It puts you in a never-ending, unfulfilling race.

ACTION HACK

Banish comparisons—first from your family and then from wherever you can! Imagine if comparisons went out of your and your children's lives—what would be possible for you and for them?

Practise

1. YOU are YOU
2. YOU are unique
3. YOU are no-limit

14

FINDING BALANCE

In today's high-pressure environment, striking the right balance between being a 'great' parent and having a 'great' career is not just stressful, but leaves most of us unfulfilled. The chapter shifts the context of parenting and provides real-life strategies to create quality time in your current schedule.

'I don't get to spend enough time with my children.'

'I think I am missing out on the best times of their life.'

'I feel career and time with children cannot be managed—either career or time with children would get compromised.'

'I feel guilty of not spending time with them.'

'I would have done a better "job" with them had I been at home.'

We hear these all the time.

One of the myths parents live with is that they don't get enough time with their children. We hear them complain about this all the time. With both parents now working in most cases—at least in urban areas—there has been a shift from our times, when one parent—usually the mother—was at home through the day. This is not to say that those times were better or that child-rearing is—or should be—primarily the mother's responsibility.

The fact that our mothers were so involved with us has created a model for us to follow through with our children. Let me explain this. For example, if my mom was a homemaker and she was available for me when I came back from school, was available to take me to wherever I wanted to go, be it hobby classes, tuitions, or was just there during examination, provided I liked it, I would want my children to get the same kind of time from their mother. In case that didn't work for me, or if I felt that she never got her due, I may not want it for my children's mother.

These are certain limiting thoughts that unconsciously drive the conversations around time with children and career options, especially for mothers.

The last couple of decades have been witness to mothers stepping out to work, just like fathers. This has not only had a positive impact on the financial situation of such families, but the exposure thus gained by mothers has also contributed to the children's mental and emotional growth. A working mother influences the outlook of the children and the family as a whole.

The other side of the story is that with both parents working in demanding jobs or as entrepreneurs, both of which require massive time and energy commitment, the amount of time they spend with children has certainly gone down. This quantitative reduction in the time spent with children often leads to a feeling of guilt, especially among mothers. This is because of their social conditioning that the child-rearing responsibilities are primarily theirs. Whenever a child's performance, behaviour or attitude is not as per expectations, people often tend to hold the mother responsible. Even when parents go to their children's school, the teachers advise the mothers to spend more time with the children. A working mother is therefore unlikely to find any time for herself—whatever time she is left with outside of work and other responsibilities, she is likely to spend on the child to reduce the guilt.

I have some good news and some bad news for you. Let me give you the bad news first. The bad news is that we have we a fixed amount of time—that a day has 24 hours, is a constant. A full-time job in our country varies between eight to nine hours; add to it a couple of hours for the daily commute and six to eight hours of sleep, and we are left with very little time to complete our other daily chores and spend time with the children.

Now the good news, which may sound illogical or even like a lie: good parenting, which reflects itself in your children doing well, you having a great relationship with them, and them being happy, healthy, responsible and unstoppable in their life, has nothing to do with the amount of time you spend with them. Parenting needs time, but good parenting is not a factor of the amount of time you spend. How you spend the time, rather than how much time you spend, is the key to good parenting.

BEFORE MOVING AHEAD ...

Think of what would you consider as 'quality time' for yourself. Revisit in your thoughts, such times from the last one week. Think of the time when you were at peace with yourself. It could be a moment spent alone or with someone else. It could be time you spent doing some activity, or doing nothing in particular. This could be a time when you were fully present in the moment, without thinking of the past or worrying about the future.

So, quality time for you is the time that you enjoyed by spending it experiencing life in the present and by yourself.

Let's discover what we mean by this, and how we can make a real difference to our and our children's lives.

The first shift we need to bring in our lives, in our day-to-day interactions with children, in our understanding of parenting, is the shift from

There is no time. ━━━━━➤ There is time; let me find it.

This shift is essential before we begin learning to find time in our current schedules. Accept the possibility of finding time.

What contributes to good parenting is what we often hear being referred to as 'quality time'. What is quality time? Every educator, advisor, coach or mentor has their own definition for the term.

Now that you understand how to identify what constitutes as 'quality time' for your own self, the next step is to figure out how to do so for your child. It may sound difficult—even complicated—but it is quite simple. All you need to do is have a chat with your child and ask them. Moreover, observe them in moments when they may not express themselves in words, but there are non-verbal manifestations of how they are feeling.

There is a misconception that quality time with the child should necessarily involve something productive, something that will add to their learning, something that gives them exposure to 'good' things such as reading, watching an informative programme, a do-it-yourself kit and so on. In reality, though, quality time is the time you spend with your child, when nothing else except you and them exists— which is to say a time when you are fully present in the moment and your entire focus is on them. This could even be watching their favourite cartoon with them, playing cards or other games, jumping on the bed, pillow fights, singing along or just being with each other, chatting, talking about your day/their day and so on. It is this quality time—even if it's in small pockets of 15 minutes a day—that your child will remember and cherish forever.

Having now understood what quality time means, let's do a small exercise. Go over your daily schedule. It may look something like this:

- Wake-up time
- Time I take to get my child ready for school
- Time I take to get ready
- Time spent commuting to work
- Work hours
- Commute from office to home
- Rest time
- Time spent with children—maybe checking their homework, taking updates about school and the day
- Time spent preparing dinner
- Time spent eating dinner
- Time spent in putting them to bed

The weekend schedule may involve additional things, such as:

- Doing household chores
- Buying vegetables, groceries and other household purchases

- Coordinating repairs and other miscellaneous work at home
- Getting together with friends or relatives and other social obligations

Now, identify the pockets of time that you can spend with your children. For instance, there may be certain activities that, if done with the children, will allow you to spend some time with them. Take the children along when you go to buy groceries. As you prepare dinner, try and involve the child in setting up the dining table, perhaps even take their help in tossing up a salad—needless to say, the complexity of the tasks needs to be mapped to the child's age.

Monica and I used this approach of spending quality time with children to solve a problem we were facing with our son Aman. When Aman was around five years old, our mornings were chaotic. The alarm would go off every morning, triggering a set of actions. 'Aman, wake up!' was a chant that Monica and I would take turns at. Irrespective of whether it was Monica's or my turn to get Aman ready for school, we would meet with the same response to our attempts at waking him up: 'Five minutes more,' he would mumble, still sleepy. After around 10 minutes of negotiation, we would force him out of his bed and send him off to the washroom. Ten minutes later, we would bang on the washroom door. More often than not he would have either dozed off sitting on the pot or was simply daydreaming! And then came the bath time. Since Aman loved water—he still does—getting him out of his bath would be another ordeal. At times, it appeared that we were denying him the things he enjoyed the most.

Even as Monica and I took turns to get Aman ready for school, when it came to dressing him up, it was always a joint effort. With only seven minutes left for the bus to arrive, we invariably ended up sending SOS cries to each other! Monica would be buttoning up Aman's shirt while I put on his socks and shoes.

All the rush allowed for only a three-minute breakfast time, when we would be literally shoving some sandwich or eggs down his throat before taking him to the bus stop. As we rushed there, we would heave a sigh of relief if we could see someone standing there—it indicated that we hadn't missed the bus, not that day. And that seemed like a big victory—one that deserved celebration in the calm post the chaos, with a hot cup of tea!

This was our daily routine—or should we say battle—for months. Then one day, both Monica and I started to chat about it. We didn't want this to continue for another 12 years—and longer, if we were to have another child (which we did). We asked others in the hope that we would find some solutions, but everyone was experiencing the same level of morning chaos as us—and they all felt it was normal.

Another thing that struck us was the paradox of spending 45 minutes with Aman every morning, but not being able to enjoy that time. It was like finding time and yet not being able to utilize it for strengthening the parent–child bond. This realization prompted us to try transforming the morning chaos into quality time with Aman. We decided that instead of taking turns to get Aman ready for school, both Monica and I would collaborate on the task every day. Then we decided to do some backward planning on the timelines and to involve Aman in this exercise. This is how our conversation went:

Monica: Aman, what time do you need to reach the bus stop to catch the bus?

Aman: 7.15 a.m.

Monica: How much time do you think it would take for us to walk to the bus stop?

Aman: Five minutes.

Me: So, we need to start from our house at 7:10 a.m.

Monica: How much time do you need to have your breakfast in peace?

Aman: Ten minutes.

Me: How much time do you need to wear your clothes at your own pace?

Aman: 15 minutes.

Monica: So that means you need to start wearing your school uniform by 6:45 a.m.

Monica: How much time do you want for taking a bath and going through your morning ablutions?

Aman: Twenty-five minutes—Ten minutes for my bath and 15 minutes on the pot!

Monica: That brings us to 6:20 a.m. How much time do you need to laze around after waking up?

Aman: Ten minutes. Can you play with me in the morning?

Me: You want to play in the morning?

Aman: Yes, it would be a good start and I would wake up and be fresh if I play for a while. Can we play a bit of cricket in the morning with the plastic ball, in the gallery?

Me: Sure! Let's do that. How much time do we need for that?

Aman: 15 minutes.

Me: Done. (There was excitement in my voice, as I too wanted some time to play with him and the thought of playing first thing in the morning was exciting.)

Monica: Great, from tomorrow onwards, we will wake you up at 6 a.m., take five minutes to laze around and 15 minutes to play before you start to get ready.

Our lives changed from that day. Both Monica and I would get up at 6 a.m., wake up Aman, and then take turns to play with him. There would be music playing in the background. Aman suddenly had more time to go through the morning tasks at his pace. At 7:10 a.m., we both would go to drop him to at the bus stop. After Vaanya was born, we would even take her along to the bus stop, making it a family affair. At the bus stop, too, we would play with the ball, till the time the bus arrived.

The new approach proved to be transformational for the family. We started looking forward to the morning time—it became our family fun time. Aman's day started with fun and excitement, and this became quality time for us to bond. When Vaanya grew up, she automatically started following the same routine—morning chaos had clearly become a thing of the past.

There is a possibility that some families may need a few iterations before reaching the comfort of the morning routine that we did. But once you figure this out, it will make a real difference in your and your child's life.

15

SCREEN DETOX

The use of the internet, computers, smartphones and other electronic devices has dramatically increased over recent decades, and this increase is associated not only with clear and tremendous benefits to the users, but also with documented cases of excessive use which often has negative health consequences. In many countries, the problem has reached the magnitude of a significant public health concern.

The World Health Organization (WHO) has included gaming disorder in the International Classification of Diseases (ICD). Gaming disorder is defined in the eleventh revision of the ICD (ICD-11) as a 'pattern of gaming behaviour ("digital-gaming" or "video-gaming") characterized by impaired control over gaming, increasing priority given to gaming over other activities to the extent that gaming takes precedence over other interests and daily activities, and continuation or escalation of gaming despite the occurrence of negative consequences.'*

I, personally, would rate this menace as more dangerous than substance abuse, simply because:

- It is legal.
- We as parents and adults not only introduce it to our

---

*https://www.who.int/features/qa/gaming-disorder/en/

children but also provide these gadgets as gifts and rewards!

The world is going digital for everything, and smartphones have become an integral part of our lives—more like extensions of our bodies. Smartphones have even been rated by some as the number one invention in the history of humankind, in terms of being the one invention that has made the maximum impact.

Most of us have been on the receiving end of this phenomena with respect to our children getting hooked on these and spending far more time on them than it is physically, mentally and emotionally healthy for them. I am sure at some point each one of you would have, either through amicable discussions or through force, tried to control/manage your child's screen time. Some of us would have succeeded and some of us would have failed and given up. Some of us would have spoken to other parents or to school teachers but more often than not would have relented, considering it's a menace that's hard to counter.

Policing screen time is exhausting—tracking usage and then clamping down on excesses can be exasperating and adversely affect the parent–child bond. We end up appearing as villains in our children's lives! Since it is almost impossible to amicably reach a point where the parent controls the screen time, let us dismantle the issue and see how we can create a win-win situation for our children—a solution where they are not only able to see that excessive use is harmful for them, but also start managing their screen time themselves.

The first step is to understand its impact on our children. There is, of course, the harmful impact of this takeover of our children's lives by technology and gadgets:

- The children are becoming averse to reading and writing.
- Outdoor activities have gone down.
- The largely sedentary lives that children have started leading impact their physical health; lack of stamina and health issues like obesity have become more common.
- Virtual lives are overpowering the in-person interactions.
- Fewer in-person interactions adversely impact their emotional quotient—ability to understand each other, manage emotions and socializing skills.
- Excessive time spent on mobiles and other gadgets is essentially time spent away from other activities like studying, pursuing hobbies, spending time with the family, etc.
- In contrast to the virtual world, studies start appearing as boring and children tend to lose interest.
- With easy access to porn on the internet, even young children are getting exposed to it. The experimentation with sex at an early age puts their health (physical and mental) at a huge risk.
- The psychological impact of not enough likes or followers on social media platforms such as Facebook and Instagram can be devastating.
- Exposure to fast-moving, attractive action is reducing their attention spans. Incidences of attention deficit hyperactivity disorder (ADHD) are increasing at an alarming rate.
- Easy access to solutions on the internet is obviating the need to think and develop problem-solving skills.

- Peer pressure has increased manifold—from who owns the latest model of a gadget to comparisons of the lives made public by people on social media (where they dined, travelled, etc.), it creates tremendous pressure on our children (and also on parents!)

Apart from the issues listed above, these gadgets and applications, by making everything available to us instantaneously—from online shopping to ordering food and booking tickets—are training our minds to expect 'instant gratification'. The fact of life, however, is that important things like love, relationships, career, etc. do not come instantaneously—they take time and effort to build. We have to go through the grind, the ups and downs and build the tenacity to passionately go after these and build them slowly, brick by brick. With the advent of gadgets, smartphones and automation, our children are not getting enough exposure and training towards building their tenacity, and this affects their ability to sustain themselves through long periods of 'boredom', 'sadness', 'loneliness' etc. in order to build their experience of satisfaction and fulfilment.

With pleasure being mistaken for happiness, society is witnessing an increased rate of breakups and divorces, and frequent changing of jobs and lines of businesses. If results don't come fast enough in personal or professional lives, people tend to lose interest and move on without investing too much time, effort and energy.

The damage done by screens can be gauged from the fact that the brain scans of a person addicted to drugs are similar to the brain scans of a person addicted to screens!

One, however, cannot ignore the unparalleled benefits of these gadgets and applications. Some of the advantages are:

- They allow for instant communication, which can help manage security risks.
- Communication is bringing people closer, albeit virtually.
- Health emergencies are being handled on the go, saving so many lives.
- Online shopping and instant availability of food, travel bookings, medical reports, etc. have made our lives comfortable and convenient.
- World trade, financial transactions, banking etc. are being facilitated.
- Business communications have become much easier.

We've come to a point in time when smartphones and other gadgets have become indispensable to our and our children's lives.

To dismantle this issue of technology overpowering our lives, we need to break the myth that children are addicted to smartphones, games and gadgets. They are not—and let us do a quick exercise to understand this statement.

When you were in your pre-teens or early teens, say between the ages of 12 and 15, what was the one activity that you were really interested in? It could be playing a sport, dancing, singing, painting, reading, roaming around with friends or something else. Close your eyes and give yourself a minute to go back into the experience of these activities at that time.

What did you get out of indulging in those activities? Write down some of your experiences being immersed in these activities. Do not analyse the benefits. Do not start writing that we learnt teamwork, physical fitness, etc. We didn't do these activities to be physically fit or practise teamwork—these kinds of skills got nurtured as side-effects. The things I got from playing cricket with my friends in the park opposite our house were as follows:

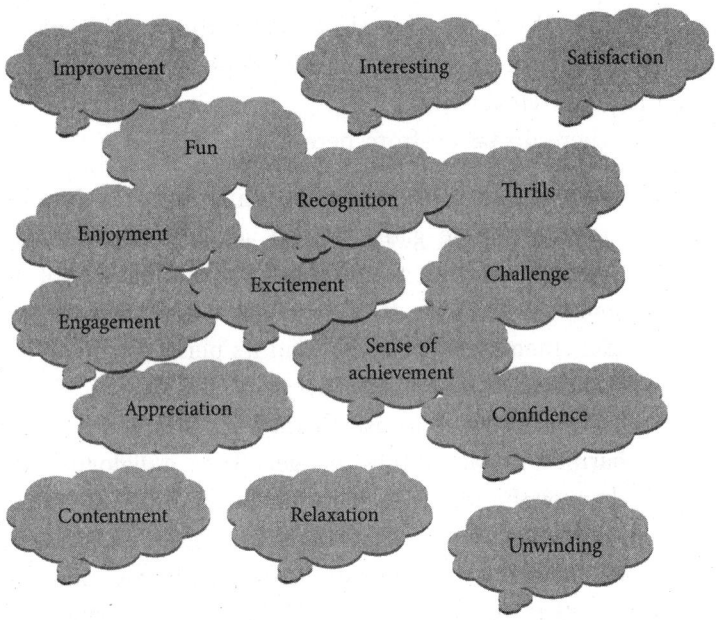

It used to be great fun. We would wait for the time to start off. At times we would lie to our parents that we had finished our homework, lest they stopped us from going out to play. We felt good when a friend appreciated our performance on the field; it gave us a sense of achievement and satisfaction that perhaps was missing for some of us at school. The time spent on the playing field was the best time of the day, as we had no one telling us what to do and how to do it, and no one 'senior' pointed out our mistakes.

The fact is that even children today look for the same

kind of things—engagement, thrill, appreciation, etc. Largely unstructured activities give us the time to unwind, just be ourselves without the pressures of performance (though there is the urge to perform better, but it is not by compulsion) or being watched, and in today's times, the time spent on smartphones and gaming has replaced playing outdoors as the unstructured activity.

So, where do we go from here?

- The first step towards supporting our children in managing these gadgets is to acknowledge, and get them to also understand, that they are hooked not on smartphones, gadgets or gaming, but on the action and excitement these provide—and it's perfectly fine to get addicted to these experiences.
- The next step is to ask them what they think is the harmful impact of these gadgets. Have a dialogue with them on this topic. During your conversation with them, remember we are not making the games and gadgets the villains; we are only discussing their pros and cons.
- The next step is to ask them if they want to suffer from the harmful impact that you have discussed. Don't be surprised if they say 'No'. They are truly not fine with the harm caused by these—they only don't know how to escape from the trap they have got into.

Once you have reached this point of agreement, you need to support your children in managing their screen time such that they are able to make the most of it in terms of engagement and entertainment, and yet know where to draw the line. For this, identify other activities that will allow them the same takeaways as their screen time gave them—fun, excitement, engagement, enjoyment, appreciation, etc.* Add these activities to their daily schedule.

Do not talk about reducing screen time! Talk about adding another activity that provides them with fun, enjoyment, excitement, recognition, appreciation etc. Adding this activity will automatically reduce the time available for screens.

A critical factor while drawing up such a list is 'availability'. Smartphones and gadgets are readily available and if your alternatives have to counter the child's screen time, they too need to be readily available in their daily routine. The transition wouldn't be smooth, simply because the ease of availability and usage of the gadgets are far superior to any other activity.

But after the initial push, the children will soon enjoy the new activities and their screen time will gradually reduce. The idea is not to ask them to reduce their screen time, but to simply provide alternatives that meet the same needs.

Many of you may disagree with the feasibility of this suggestion. You may say that you have already tried putting your child in coaching classes for sports or art or music and dance, but it didn't work. They lost interest and dropped out. Did you put them into those things without having a dialogue with them? Don't miss out on that critical step. Moreover, coaching classes for the things that your child may otherwise love and enjoy end up making those very activities structured—they become more about technique, and even competitive, rather than activities that help them unwind. With their performance being monitored in such classes, they often have the same anxiety levels as, say,

---

*https://www.youtube.com/watch?v=9Hms8mF5nyM&t=35s

school classes. So, remember two critical things for such activities:

- It has to be FREE time.
- It has to be unstructured.*

Do you remember that when we were involved in such fun activities in our childhood, no one was watching us, no one was instructing us? We were free to do our own thing.

If you are considering a structured activity, such as dance classes or sports coaching, do it when the child wants to get better and improve their skills.

ACTION HACK

- Create a rule of no screens during meal time.
- Meal times are family times—chat, talk about the day, crack jokes, share your childhood stories, listen to your children's stories.
- Do not carry more than one phone (just in case there is an emergency) when dining out. It's the time to be with each other and have some fun together. It's the time to socialize in person, and not on social media.
- Take up a hobby for yourself. It's never too late to indulge in the activities we love.

---

*https://www.youtube.com/watch?v=9Hms8mF5nyM&t=35s

16

EATING HEALTHY

One of the biggest challenges faced by parents today is to get their children to eat healthy home-cooked meals. They seem to detest eating veggies, especially green veggies and healthy home-cooked food. In fact, healthy eating habits are a challenge for parents themselves too.

Let's try to dismantle this issue by way of an exercise. To begin with, answer the following question:

- Whose need is it to eat?[**]

The answer to this is quite simple. It is the child's need. Now, review your daily actions and discussions to assess whether it has remained the child's need, or whether you have made it your need. The following questions would help you decipher this for yourself:

- Who is after them to eat?
- Who ensures that they eat well and eat on time?
- Who gets bothered if they don't eat proper meals?
- Who is worried about including fruits, milk and vegetables in their diet?
- Who gets upset if they sleep off without eating?

[**]https://www.youtube.com/watch?v=1DVKFVIfaDc&t=1s

- In case they throw a tantrum, who runs after them to feed them?
- Who doesn't eat if the child doesn't eat?

If the answer to even two of these questions is 'I' or 'my spouse', then your child having food has become *your* need, rather than theirs. Before you try to counter this, let's examine the question 'Whose need is it?' closely.

The need for oxygen, food and water are survival needs. These needs are not dependent on any individual. Every living organism on this planet needs these to survive, and survival is a basic instinct and not an acquired skill. A living being's survival instinct is independent of age, maturity or any training. Even before a child is born, it draws nutrition in the mother's womb to survive. With this understanding will come the realization that as parents we need to provide food to our children till the time they can take care of themselves, but they will only eat the food when they are hungry. Their hunger will make that food their need. Step back from trying to feed them.

This transition would not be easy, because it means breaking a cycle reinforced through the years. It will not only be difficult for you as parents, but may ruffle some feathers at the other end too. The child is likely to throw tantrums, and these could be far more intense than their earlier ones. They may not eat what you cooked or served them, they may ask for 'junk' food, ask for you to feed them, go to sleep without eating (this one works the best in triggering off the emotions of the parent to a level where more often than not the parent gives in), throw the food plate, cry, complain to others in the family and so on.

You can draw your strength from two things:

- Eating is a basic survival instinct of every living being. So, your child *will* eat. They cannot control hunger beyond a point. (If, however, you suspect a medical condition, please consult a medical practitioner.)
- Your job is to make them responsible for their life. They have to learn to fend for themselves and this is a critical step in your parenting. Your job is not complete till the time you are able to hand over the reins of their life in their hands.

A lot of thoughts may be running through your minds right now. Will this work? I have tried this before and it did not work—I had to give in after a couple of hours; my spouse came in and fed the child; we had a huge fight; my parents/in-laws accused me of being cruel; my son/daughter started calling me a bad mom.

Alternatively, you may belong to the other group of parents who would say—I love to feed my child; it gives me pleasure and satisfaction. It feels good when I feed them with my own hands; it's such a fulfilling experience. When I feed them, they have a wholesome meal. At this point, you need to revisit the question 'Whose need is it?' If you hear your own answers/responses carefully, you would find that these responses are emanating from you considering this as your need.

However, once you do understand that your role is limited to providing food and that you need to empower them to become responsible for their own life in time, the second step is to really understand what they are getting out of eating unhealthy food. Go through this evaluation process with yourself first and then also with your child.

What do they get from eating junk food? Listen to them:

- It is tasty
- One feels good while eating it
- A sense of enjoyment
- A feeling of happiness or pleasure
- Satiates hunger
- 'I had pizza last night!' makes for great conversation with friends

The Problem of Junk Food Consumption

The dark side of junk food is not unknown. Several research studies have shown that fast foods and processed foods have increased the rate of childhood obesity, heart disease, diabetes and other chronic diseases. Recently, the Delhi government demanded a crackdown on junk food being sold within 50 metres of schools. Not only do unhealthy options add inches to your waistline, studies conducted by scientists and researchers have also indicated that junk food can actually cause serious damage to your brain. The worrying bit is that it's not just years of poor eating—regular consumption of junk food even for a few days can lead to a mental meltdown.

In his book, *Encyclopedia of Junk Food and Fast Food*, Andrew F. Smith defines junk food as 'those commercial products, including candy, bakery goods, ice cream, salty snacks, and soft drinks, which have little or no nutritional value but do have plenty of calories, salt, and fats. While not all fast foods are junk foods, most are. Fast foods are ready-to-eat foods served promptly after ordering.'

The more junk food you consume, the less likely you are to consume the essential nutrients that your body relies on for growth and basic functioning. You know that junk food can hurt your health, but you may have not known about the effects of junk food on the functioning of your brain.

Memory and Learning Problems

A study published in the *American Journal of Clinical Nutrition* in 2011 showed that healthy people who ate junk food daily for only five days performed poorly on cognitive tests that measured attention, speed and mood.[*] It concluded that eating junk food regularly for five days can deteriorate your memory. This probably stems from the fact that a poor or toxic diet can cause certain chemical reactions that lead to inflammation in the hippocampus area of the brain, which is associated with memory and special recognition.

Diets that are high on sugar and fat can suppress the activity of a brain peptide called BDNF (brain-derived neurotrophic factor) that helps with learning and memory formation. Moreover, the brain contains synapses that are responsible for learning and memory. Eating too many calories can interfere with the healthy production and functioning of these synapses.

Dementia

Increase in the risk of dementia is one of the scariest discoveries associated with the consumption of junk food. You may know that insulin is produced in the pancreas and helps in the transportation of glucose to fuel the body. Insulin is also produced in the brain, where it helps in carrying signals

*Silvia Scaglioni, Chiara Arrizza, Fiammetta Vecchi, Sabrina Tedeschi. 'Determinants of children's eating behavior'. *The American Journal of Clinical Nutrition*, Volume 94, Issue 6, December 2011, Pages 2006S–2011S, https://doi.org/10.3945/ajcn.110.001685

between nerve cells and forming memories. A study conducted at the Brown University shows that too much fatty food and sweets can substantially increase the insulin levels in our body.

Reduced Ability to Control Appetite

Excess consumption of trans fats found in fried and processed foods can send mixed signals to the brain, which makes it difficult for the brain to process what you have eaten and how hungry you are. This is probably why you end up overeating. Healthy brain functions require a daily dose of essential fatty acids like omega-6 and omega-3. Deficiency of these two elements increases the risk of attention deficit disorder, dementia, bipolar disorder, and other brain-related problems.

Overconsumption of junk food may displace these with trans fats, which are harder to digest. A 2011 study shows that trans fats may cause inflammation in the hypothalamus, the part of the brain that contains neurons which control body weight. In a worst-case scenario, the habit of overeating can take proportions similar to drug addiction—with junk foods activating the pleasure centres of the brain.

A lot of studies have shown that eating foods high on sugar and fats actually changes the chemical activity of the brain, making it more dependent on such foods. A study conducted at the University of Montreal on mice showed that they suffered withdrawal symptoms after their regular junk food diet was discontinued. In humans, these withdrawal symptoms can give way to an inability to deal with stress and make you feel depressed, and eventually you would turn back to those foods to comfort yourself and manage these feelings. Soon enough, you may be caught in a vicious cycle. Moreover, by consuming too much fast food you may lose out on essential nutrients like the amino acid tryptophan, the lack of which can increase the probability of depression. An imbalance of fatty acids is another reason why people who consume more junk food are at a higher risk of depression.

Uncontrollable Cravings and Impatience

Eating a sugary cupcake or doughnut may temporarily spike your blood sugar levels, making you feel happy and satisfied, but as soon as they return to normal you are left feeling all the more irritable.

Fast food is packed with refined carbohydrates, which cause your blood sugar levels to fluctuate rapidly. If your sugar levels dip too low, it can cause anxiety, confusion and fatigue. With high content of sugar and fats, you tend to eat too fast and too much to satisfy your cravings. This can set off impatient behaviour while dealing with other things. Fast foods and processed foods may be laden with artificial flavourings and preservatives like sodium benzoate, which tend to increase hyperactivity.

Now, if we look at it, there are certain perceived 'benefits' of having junk food, as listed above, and this is also a huge health hazard. I am sure that you have been telling your child(ren) about the harmful effects of 'junk' food, but that normally doesn't have an impact on them. They still ask for it, demand it, throw a tantrum for it—and ultimately they do end up consuming it!

The pull towards the pleasure of taste is too high. This pull holds for us as much as for them—at a certain level we too give in to tastes. Advertisements that have the power to influence, easy availability and the pleasure of taste are together too attractive for a child to counter.

Moreover, when we talk of the adverse impact of eating junk food, the fact is that these negative effects on our body and mind take time to show up. But they instantaneously satiate hunger in a way that our palate enjoys. This difference in the timing of the contrasting impacts hinders children's ability to see these food items as being hazardous to health. As children tend to think of only the immediate impact of these food items—that they will enjoy and relish a meal that comprises of such items—leads to altercations and tantrums, and as parents we tend to give in simply because such moments can be exhausting.

Let me ask you a question. Would you give in if your child were to throw tantrums about drugs? This is an extreme example, but I want to drive home the point that, essentially, junk food too hampers their health—albeit at a slower pace than drugs and perhaps not as intensely—and yet we tend to give in easily.

Let's not underestimate the damage of junk food on our and our children's health. Let the convenience of takeout food not make us turn a blind eye to the damage such food is causing—damage which is not immediately visible, but imminent nonetheless. While it would be ideal to completely shun junk food and encourage healthy eating habits, it may be difficult to do so right away. So, start taking small steps towards that ultimate goal. Be firm with your child; reduce their access to these foods by not stocking kitchen cabinets and refrigerators with them. Learn to pay attention to what your children—and even you—eat. Understand the importance of reading labels on packaged food. And most importantly, don't get bullied into giving in to their tantrums. Tantrums are expected, especially if they have had access to junk food earlier. Never lose track of the fact that you are curtailing their access to junk food for their own benefit. Sometimes children need tough love too.*

The next stage would be to reach a point where the child learns to manage their intake of junk food without constant supervision and enforcement from the parents. One can reach this stage only by adopting a collaborative approach, so that the child feels involved in the process. Have a conversation with your child. Remember that the journey to reach the point where the child takes complete responsibility of their intake of unhealthy food is iterative, and it may not be easy from the start. It is all about reinforcing the behaviour till it becomes a habit. Don't stop midway thinking, I have tried already and the result has not been what I wanted. If you were to doubt the very existence of the destination midway through your journey and withdraw, you would never reach it. You need to keep on the path.

For first-timers, I normally recommend putting the process in front and diligently checking off the steps, lest you miss out.

Step zero for the process is to set the context. This needs to be done at 'peace time'—that is, when no altercation over food or anything else is in progress. Do it when everyone is relaxed—over a weekend, sitting around a table or perhaps even out in the park. Define the problem statement not in terms of junk food alone, but the harmful impact of junk food on health and the altercations it leads to within the family. Articulate, collaboratively with your child, the problem.

Whenever we ask parents what the real problem is with their children's eating habits, the usual responses are:

---

*https://www.youtube.com/watch?v=Wzh_2RaqAeo

- They eat a lot of junk food.
- They do not eat healthy food.
- They do not eat veggies.
- I have to keep following up with them and run after them to eat.

A closer look would reveal that what they state as the problem is not the real issue; they are simply articulating what happens. We need to delve deeper to find the real problem. For instance, let's look at the first case: They eat a lot of junk food.

> *What's the problem in their eating a lot of junk food?*
> They then don't eat healthy food.
> *What's the problem if they don't eat healthy food?*
> This is damaging for their health.
> *Now that is the real problem.*

We normally don't delve deep enough to identify the real problem, and so our solutions too are mapped to the superficial problem identified by us. Even when, in our head, we want our children to eat healthy because we know that in the long run junk food would be damaging for them—physically, mentally and emotionally—we don't talk about the damage; we simply insist they stop eating junk food. Without proper reasoning behind our asking them to do so, they respond the way they do. They like the taste and the food is satiating their hunger; so, essentially it meets the two purposes of food, as they see it.

It is, therefore, very important to first identify the real problem. Before you talk to the child, step back and ask yourself the question 'What is the problem?' at least thrice—the idea behind this is that the delay will help you arrive at the real problem.

Once you have articulated the problem statement, the next step would be to share your needs and feelings on the issue and have your child do the same.

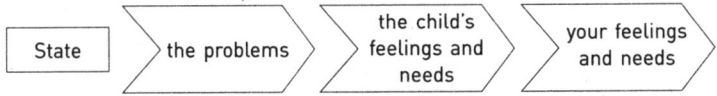

Figure 3. Working Things Out Together

Give the child the opportunity to share their feelings and needs on the matter before you share your own needs. Moreover, it is important to just listen to them and not disagree with or counter what they say.

- How does the child feel
- What are their needs around junk food
- Why they like it so much
- Why they want it
- What happens to them when they eat it

Once the child has shared all they have to say, it is your turn to share your needs and feelings. Ask them to hear you out without responding—just as you did for them.

At this point, you are only trying to understand each other's perspective on the issue. Understand; do not judge, argue or counter anything the other person says. You may want to take notes, as that would also help you focus on things that don't give you too much space to analyse, judge or respond—simply record what is being said. Use the feelings wheel extensively during these discussions.

While the child can—and should—use this opportunity to share how junk food is a way of satiating hunger that also brings them joy, as a parent, you may want to share the harmful impact of junk food and your exasperation at not being able to control it, and so also its impact on your own child's health.

The next step is to brainstorm solutions. At this stage too, do not judge; simply listen to solutions suggested by others and share your own recommendations. Record all suggestions in writing and then, together, analyse them one at a time. Strike off the ones on which there is consensus that they lack feasibility.

Once you arrive at a shorter list of solutions, go through each item on the list together as a family and see how you can build a process. Through this collaborative process you would have arrived at a solution that would be better than the situation you are in currently.

The next step is to fix up an implementation plan—what actions to take, who needs to take them, and timelines.

At times, the solution you arrive at in discussion with the family may be something that you have tried before, which hadn't worked then. Even in such a case, refrain from thinking it wouldn't work this time. The process isn't complete and it is best to not arrive at such conclusions in haste.

The next step is to arrive at deterrents.

As we discussed earlier, the adverse impact of eating junk food is not immediately palpable; it takes years for the ill-effects of eating food lacking nutrition to start showing in our body. Therefore, to ensure that we don't end up in that state in the future, we need to think of deterrents that would stop us from indulging in junk food.

First, let's understand what a deterrent is.

deterrent

Dictionary result for deterrent
noun: **deterrent**; plural noun: **deterrents**
1. a thing that discourages or is intended to discourage someone from doing something.
   'cameras are a major **deterrent to** crime'
   synonyms: disincentive, discouragement, dissuasion, damper, brake, curb, check, restraint;
   antonyms: incentive, encouragement Adjective: **deterrent**
1. able or intended to deter.
   'the deterrent effect of heavy prison sentences'

In simple terms, deterrents are things that will stop us from doing something we promised we wouldn't. Or, in other words, they will help us do what we said we would. For instance, if we fail to do what we just agreed, they would be certain deterrents which would be applied. For instance, if you agree to not bringing certain food items home and yet you still do, a deterrent could be to throw such food items into the dustbin even if this means losing the money spent on them. So, in this case, the loss of money is a deterrent for us in bringing such food items home. For every action, fix up a deterrent. Do not ignore this step, as it is critical for the effectiveness of the process.

You may argue and you may have your child resist this step and call it a punishment. This is not a punishment. It is important for both you and your child to understand the difference between punishment and deterrent:

- Unlike punishments, deterrents are co-created before the action happens.

- Deterrents are results of actions taken or not taken, as the case may be.
- You as a parent are just applying a deterrent; the cause, and so the responsibility, lies with the child.

It's critical to have a deterrent that is

- **Implementable:** Do not fix something that you will not be able to implement. Most parents make the mistake of keeping deterrents like 'we will not talk to you for a period of time'. While that may sound significant, it is something that would be difficult to implement.
- **Big enough to deter:** The stakes should be high enough for everyone to keep their promise.

The next step would be to fix up the implementation schedule—the actions that needs to be taken, who needs to take the actions, and the timelines for the actions need to be determined. The last step is very critical and yet it is often missed—setting a review date. This could be a strenuous process to follow for the first few times. There would be a lot of negotiations, agreements and disagreements. However, things will become easier as you move along. Moreover, the review would give you the chance to revisit the process and the arrangements. It would allow you to make changes that would help increase the effectiveness of the process. For instance, there may have been certain permutations and combinations which could not be envisaged earlier, or the deterrent could be very harsh, very lenient or not implementable. At this point, you can review and make the necessary revisions. The review step must not be skipped even if everything is going as per plan—it will give you the opportunity to reinforce the things that are working well. Also, take this as an opportunity to appreciate your child and yourself for the good work.

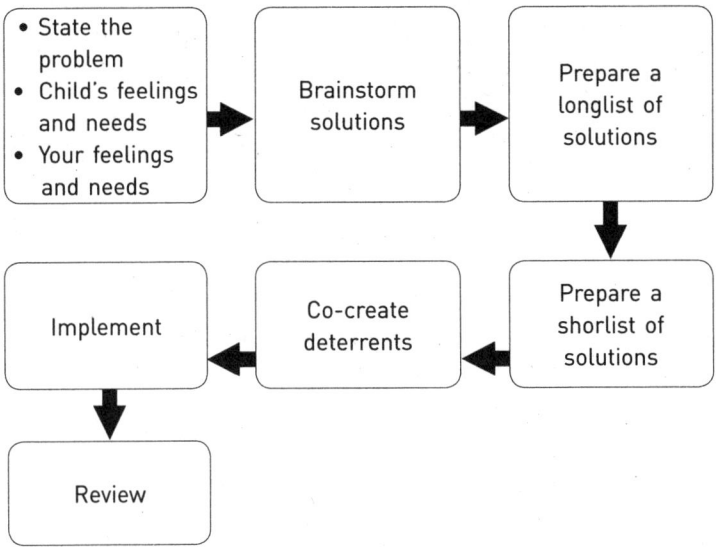

Renu, as it goes with most parents, was dealing with the issue of managing the intake of junk food for her children. Junk food consumption for both her daughters, Ria and Ahana, had increased over the last couple of years and Renu was concerned about its impact on their health. With the exposure in school, it was getting very difficult to manage. They would have their friends' birthdays, where they would end up consuming junk food. Every pizza and burger company would have amazing advertisements on TV, hoardings, newspapers, etc. and it was almost impossible for Renu to keep her children away from it. Her attempts at controlling their junk food intake ended up making her a 'bad mom'. She also started hating herself for not allowing her children what brought them happiness. We recommended that she follow the process that we have explained here, and she did.

On a Saturday afternoon, we gathered the courage to ask her daughters to come and sit with her for a discussion. Their first response was: 'Mom, now don't start another round of advising! It's weekend and we don't want to get into a round of arguments.' Renu and her husband Rishi were in alignment over the issue. Rishi saw how the daughters' comment had impacted Renu, and he intervened. He told the children that this is not a parents vs children discussion, where they want to impose something on them. By this time Renu had recovered from the hurt and asked both the kids to share how they felt when she asked them to sit for a discussion. The children made a face, but Renu brought out a sheet of paper that had emoticons on them. She suggested a few feelings that she thought applied to them, and they nodded in agreement with some.

Renu acknowledged that it was fine for her children to feel so. Instead of telling them they were wrong, she shared her own feelings of being scared and lonely.

They went through the process of sharing their feelings and needs in the area of junk food. The difference was that this time both Renu and Rishi heard them out without saying anything. They could really understand that the food was far more delicious and attractive than home-cooked healthy food. And when other children in the school brought them, it became very difficult for the two girls to resist.

Once they shared that and saw neither their father nor the mother being defensive or trying to make them understand the adverse impact, both Ria and Ahana shared their side of the story completely. Once they were done, Rishi asked them if they knew the impact of this food on their health. To their surprise, both of them could articulate the impact very well. They told their parents that they had done extensive research at school while studying their chapter on balanced diet. They even knew how and why a balanced diet is critical for everyone.

All Rishi and Renu had to now do was to ask them the way out. Ria and Ahana gave an idea of fixing up two days of the week when they would have one meal of such food. The parents were so impressed by the responses of their daughters that they quickly agreed.

They agreed to Saturday and Wednesday being the junk meal days. So on such a day, they planned to go out together for pizzas. This was an amazing experience. They all had pizzas without the guilt of eating junk and with Renu relieved from the role of the monitor. She was at ease that day.

The next five days went by peacefully, with no altercations on food or meals. This was too good to be true. But hell broke loose on Thursday, when one of their friends walked in with a packet of noodles and a bucket of ice cream for the kids. It was like the kids were starving. They pounced on the food. Renu was shocked but given that the person was a guest, she couldn't say anything.

When Rishi came back from office, it was like a tigress was waiting for her prey. She poured out all that had happened along with her emotions. For her, the entire work of the last weekend and even the coaching she had gone through had broken down. This was probably her last effort to build a peaceful and trusting relationship with her daughters. She even extrapolated how this was going to impact their relationship in the future.

Post dinner, they brought out the process note to check what had gone wrong. Her coach at Parwarish had guaranteed results. And here she was in the middle of a breakdown.

While they were going through the process, they saw that they had implemented the process half way When both the children suggested a way out, which is what they had wanted, the process had been compete for them.

When they saw the process note, they realized that the steps of creating deterrents, actions, timelines and review dates weren't done.

It was time to act again. They called the kids to their room and apologized for their reaction. The children started crying and started apologizing too. They didn't realize that their breaking of the rule would lead to their mom being so upset.

They all acknowledged that the process worked for five days, without anyone following up or controlling. They had to now create deterrents. The kids also saw that their promise of setting up two days a week for a junk meal wasn't enough. They would need structures to support their promises. Renu proposed a deterrent that if they took one meal more than what they agreed on for the week, then they would forgo the junk meal days for the entire next week. Ria initially didn't want to agree because that would lead to them losing out on the two days. Ahana, the elder one, quickly added that since they were going to follow the regime, there was no question of the deterrent being applied.

The other thing they did as a family was to fix up a review day and time. 4.30 p.m. every Sunday was the time booked for a discussion between the four of them.

This process really worked for the family. It's been almost one year and junk food has become a non-contentious issue. There have been a couple of 'cheat' days. But those are one-off 'trump card' days and the family accepts them without blaming anyone. It's amazing to see how Ria and Ahana, at this young age, have taken complete responsibility of this area in their hands. Even when they came for dinner to our place on a Friday, they simply refused cold drinks, saying, 'It's our no junk day.'

I hope the case study shared here will give you the confidence that you too can get your children to adopt healthy eating. All you need to do is follow the process.

EPILOGUE:
WHAT'S THE REAL DEFINITION OF PARENTING?

A very critical part of parenting is to understand: 'What is my real role as a parent?'

I have asked this question to millions of parents by now. In response, most parents ask me what I mean.

The simple-sounding question can come across as fairly confrontational. It may appear that someone is challenging your understanding of parenting.

Let's dwell on this question for a bit. If someone was to write a job description of your role as a parent, what would it look like? In order to answer this, let us go through a typical day and see what all we do for our children:

- Waking them up for the school in the morning
- Getting them ready for school (following up from the bed to the bus through the toilet!)
- Cooking for them or making food available for them
- Feeding them (even running behind them to feed them!)
- Making them complete their homework
- Ensuring that they study for their exams
- Taking them to the hobby/sports classes (even forcing them to go at times)

- Getting them to sleep at night
- Monitoring their screen time
- Monitoring their hygiene/health habits

And the list goes on.

Just going through this list and doing the same work for years could be a very exasperating job.

Let's look at this differently to figure out a role that could be fulfilling and joyous. Let's prepare lists of items that

- your child does on their own and you don't need to follow up on them
- you have to follow up on, or even do yourself, for your children

As you prepare these lists, become aware of your experience of parenting in these areas, their experience of interactions with you, and the nature of communication between you and them. Notice how these things are diametrically opposite for these two lists.

In the areas where your child does things on their own without the need for you to follow up with them, the experience is that of peace, compassion and love, and you feel proud of them. However, in the areas where you have to constantly follow up with them (even nag them) to even make them move, the experience is exasperating. It not only leaves you feeling low and perhaps agitated, it also spoils their experience of life.

Another thing that we have observed is that different parents have had different items on either list. For some parents, eating healthy has appeared on the no follow-up list, while for others, it's been on the follow-up list. Similarly, studies, hygiene, reading habits, etc. have featured on both lists. What we want to highlight here is that it has nothing to do with the activity. The general impression is that children don't want to study on their own, they don't want to take care of their belongings on their own, they have to be followed up with to get them to maintain their own hygiene, they have to be stopped from eating junk food, or they kept away from screens. In our experience, these lists are very different for every parent. What appears on one list for one set of parents appears on the other list for another set of parents. The pattern in these lists, and the analysis of that pattern, would give you the key to solving these problems and even help you in defining your role as a parent.

Let's first see the pattern.

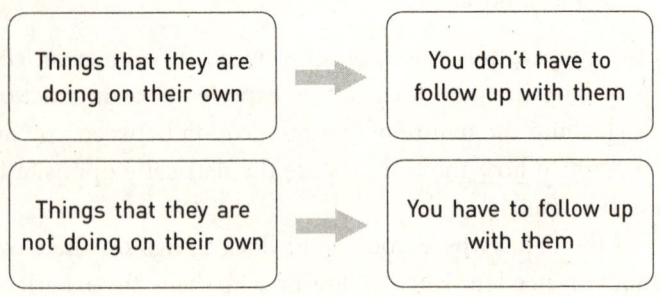

This seems to be the logical interpretation of this.

In reality, that's not the case. Examine it for yourself. What is actually happening is exactly the opposite of this.

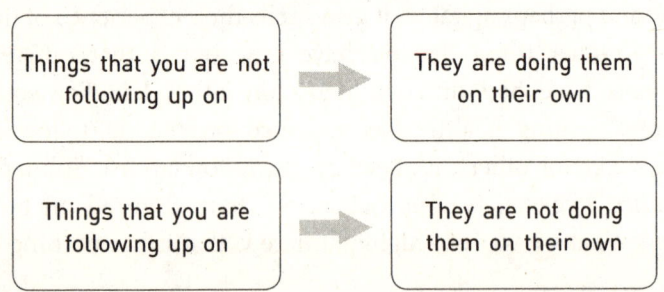

Yes, you may not believe it at first, but let's examine these lists for our own selves. Look at the areas of your life that you have taken responsibility of—you would see that your spouse is dependent on you for those, and vice versa. My request would be to really examine this for yourself in your own life. This would open up a whole new world for you.

You have great experiences in the areas where you have supported your child in taking responsibility, as their actions are almost automatic in those areas. Not just the outcome, the experience itself is amazing.

We now come to the question we started this conversation with: what is your role as a parent?

The answer to this cannot be anything but: Making your children responsible for their own lives.* That is your one-line job description as a parent.

We are not saying let them figure things out all on their own. We are saying support them in taking responsibility of their life. Start with one element at a time and start handing over the reins of their life to them. The tools given in this book would support you in doing just that. Use them extensively, and whenever you falter, come back to them. I am sure you would be able to find fulfilment and joy in day-to-day parenting, and you would be able to nurture the nolimitness of your children.

Happy Parenting!

---

*https://www.youtube.com/watch?v=IECQ88XNFQk

ACKNOWLEDGEMENTS

I take this opportunity to acknowledge each and every person who had a role in raising me—my grandparents, extended family, parents, friends, siblings, children, my teachers at school and colleges. My colleagues, peers, team members and supervisors also contributed to this book, each in their own unique way.

A special mention to Dr Wayne Dyer, whose coining of the word 'nolimit' sowed the seeds of Parwarish and our work.

The journey of Parwarish and this book would not have been possible without the unwavering support of Dad, Mom, Monica, Aman and Vaanya.

Special thanks to my team members Renuka, Sonali, Manvi, Nupur, and Saba, who not only contributed in creating and leading the 'Nolimit child programme' but also helped in putting this book together.

A big thank you to each and every member of Team Parwarish—everyone who is/was a part of the Parwarish journey at some point of time.

And finally, all the parents who trusted us and embarked on the journey of parenting the 'Parwarish way'. Their experiences and results encouraged us to put this book together for each and every parent.